The Architecture of Robert Venturi

*Essays by Vincent Scully, David Van Zanten, Neil Levine,
Thomas Beeby, and Stephen Kieran*

Edited and with an introduction by Christopher Mead

*University of New Mexico Press
Albuquerque*

Library of Congress Cataloging in Publication Data

The Architecture of Robert Venturi.

   Includes bibliographical references and index.
    1. Venturi, Robert—Criticism and interpretation.
2. Architecture, Modern—20th century—United States.
3. Architecture, Postmodern—United States.
I. Venturi, Robert.   II. Mead, Christopher, 1953–
NA737.V45A84   1989   720′.92′4   88-33889
ISBN 0-8263-1120-2
ISBN 0-8263-1121-0 (pbk.)

Second paperbound printing, 1989

Design by Mary Shapiro

Contents

Illustrations

70. Le Corbusier, Maisons Jaoul, Neuilly-sur-Seine, France, 1954–56. (Photograph: Le Corbusier, *Oeuvre Complète. Volume VI: 1952–1957,* 1957.)

71. Le Corbusier, High Court of Justice, Chandigarh, India, 1951–56. (Photograph: Le Corbusier, *Oeuvre Complète. Volume VI: 1952–1957,* 1957.)

72. Le Corbusier, Chapel of Notre-Dame-du-Haut, Ronchamp, France, 1950–55. Interior. (Photograph: Neil Levine.)

73. Frank Lloyd Wright, Morris Store, San Francisco, California, 1948–49. (Photograph: Neil Levine.)

74. Frank Lloyd Wright, Marin County Civic Center, San Rafael, California, 1957–70. (Photograph: Neil Levine.)

75. Eero Saarinen, Chapel, Massachusetts Institute of Technology, Cambridge, Massachusetts, 1951–55. (Photograph: Neil Levine.)

76. Oscar Niemeyer, Presidential Palace (Palace of the Dawn), Brasilia, Brazil, 1956–59. (Photograph: Christian Hornig, *Oscar Niemeyer. Bauten und Projekte,* 1981.)

77. Louis I. Kahn, U.S. Consulate project, Luanda, Angola, 1959. Chancellery, isometric of side wall. (Photograph: Heinz Ronner, Sharad Jhaver, Alessandro Vasella; in Louis I. Kahn, *Complete Works, 1935–74,* 1987.)

78. Louis I. Kahn, Meeting House project, Salk Institute for Biological Studies, La Jolla, California, begun 1959. Perspective. (Photograph: Collection of the Museum of Modern Art, New York. Gift of the architect.)

79. Giovanni Battista Piranesi, *Baths of Caracalla,* etching. (Photograph: Fogg Art Museum, Harvard University.)

80. Eugène-Emmanuel Viollet-le-Duc, *Analysis of Roman Baths,* lithograph, mid-1860s. (Photograph: Service Photographique de la Caisse Nationale des Monuments Historiques et des Sites.)

81. Louis I. Kahn, Library, Phillips Exeter Academy, Exeter, New Hampshire, 1965–72. (Photograph: Neil Levine.)

82. Venturi and Rauch, Vanna Venturi House, Chestnut Hill, Philadelphia, Pennsylvania, 1961–64. Front and side facades. (Photograph: Neil Levine.)

83. Louis I. Kahn, Fisher House, Hatboro, Pennsylvania, 1960. (Photograph: Neil Levine.)

84. Venturi and Rauch, with Cope and Lippincott, Guild House, Philadelphia, Pennsylvania, 1960–63. Rear facade. (Photograph: Neil Levine.)

85. Venturi and Rauch, with Cope and Lippincott, Guild House, Philadelphia, Pennsylvania, 1960–63. Corner view of rear and side facades. (Photograph: Neil Levine.)

86. Venturi and Rauch, with Cope and Lippincott, Guild House, Philadelphia, Pennsylvania, 1960–63. Front facade along Spring Garden Street. (Photograph: Neil Levine.)

87. Piazza Malphigi, Bologna, Italy. View of square, with apse of S. Francesco on the right. (Photograph: Fogg Museum of Art, Harvard University.)

88. Frank Lloyd Wright, Ward Willits House, Highland Park, Illinois, 1901–2. Plan. (Photograph: Copyright © the Frank Lloyd Wright Memorial Foundation; in H. R. Hitchcock, *In the Nature of Materials: The Buildings of Frank Lloyd Wright, 1887–1941,* 1942.)

89. Le Corbusier, Contemporary City for 3 Million People project, 1922–25. Perspective. (Photograph: Le Corbusier and P. Jeanneret, *Oeuvre Complète. Volume I: 1910–1929,* 1929.)

90. Le Corbusier, Model of the Dom-ino System, 1914. (Photograph: Le Corbusier and P. Jeanneret, *Oeuvre Complète. Volume I: 1910–1929,* 1929.)

91. Kevin Roche, John Dinkeloo and Associates, Richard C.

Lee High School, New Haven, Connecticut, 1962–67. (Photograph: Neil Levine.)

92. Moshe Safdie, Habitat, Montreal, Quebec, Canada, 1967. (Photograph: Neil Levine.)

93. Hugh Stubbins and Associates, Citicorp Center, New York, New York, 1977. (Photograph: Andrew Minchin.)

94. Street Scene in Downtown Dallas, Texas. (Photograph: Alex Webb/Magnum.)

95. Venturi, Rauch and Scott Brown, Gordon Wu Hall, Princeton University, Princeton, New Jersey, 1980–83. General view from the south. (Photograph: Neil Levine.)

96. Venturi, Rauch and Scott Brown, Gordon Wu Hall, Princeton University, Princeton, New Jersey, 1980–83. Front facade along entrance path. (Photograph: Neil Levine.)

97. Marc-Antoine Laugier, *Essai sur l'architecture,* 1755. Frontispiece.

98. Fairbanks House, Dedham, Massachusetts, 1637. (Photograph: *The American Architect and Building News,* 1881; in Abbott Lowell Cummings, *The Framed Houses of Massachusetts Bay, 1625–1725,* 1979.)

99. Nantucket, Nantucket Island, Massachusetts. (Photograph: John McCalley; courtesy of Nantucket Historical Association.)

100. Parson Capen House, Topsfield, Massachusetts, 1683. (Photograph: Sandak Inc.; in William Pierson, Jr., *American Buildings and Their Architects,* vol. 1, 1970.)

101. Two-story house, South Yarmouth, Cape Cod, Massachusetts, n.d. (Photograph: Alfred Easton Poor, *Colonial Architecture of Cape Cod, Nantucket and Martha's Vineyard,* 1932.)

102. Standish House, Halifax, Massachusetts, 1730. (Photo-

graph: The Society for the Preservation of New England Antiquities; in Virginia and Lee McAlester, *A Field Guide to American Houses,* 1984.)

103. Shingle Style house, New London, Connecticut, late nineteenth century. (Photograph: Thomas Hahn; in Virginia and Lee McAlester, *A Field Guide to American Houses,* 1984.)

104. Cape Cod Style house, Gibson County, Indiana, circa 1935. (Photograph: Virginia and Lee McAlester, *A Field Guide to American Houses,* 1984.)

105. Venturi and Rauch, Trubek House, Nantucket Island, Massachusetts, 1970–71. Elevations. (Photograph: Venturi, Rauch and Scott Brown.)

106. Venturi and Rauch, Trubek House, Nantucket Island, Massachusetts, 1970–71. Plans and sections. (Photograph: Venturi, Rauch and Scott Brown.)

107. Venturi and Rauch, Wislocki House, Nantucket Island, Massachusetts, 1970–71. Elevations, plans, and section. (Photograph: Venturi, Rauch and Scott Brown.)

108. Gable Front house, Hussey Street, Nantucket, Nantucket Island, Massachusetts, early nineteenth century. (Photograph: Henry S. Wyer; courtesy of Nantucket Historical Association.)

109. Loft houses, Old North Wharf, Nantucket, Nantucket Island, Massachusetts, 1850s. Waterfront facades. (Photograph: John McCalley; courtesy of Nantucket Historical Association.)

110. Loft houses, Old North Wharf, Nantucket, Nantucket Island, Massachusetts, 1850s. Street facades. (Photograph: John McCalley; courtesy of Nantucket Historical Association.)

111. "Auld Lang Syne," Siaconset, Nantucket Island, Massachusetts, 1675. (Photograph: H. Marshall Gardiner; courtesy of Nantucket Historical Association.)

England, 1714–17. Aisle window. (Photograph: in Kerry Downes, *Hawksmoor*, 1980.)

132. Venturi, Rauch and Scott Brown, Gordon Wu Hall, Princeton University, Princeton, New Jersey, 1980–83. Front facade from the north toward Butler Plaza. (Photograph: Elizabeth Moule.)

133. Venturi, Rauch and Scott Brown, Gordon Wu Hall, Princeton University, Princeton, New Jersey, 1980–83. Gate-entry. (Photograph: Elizabeth Moule.)

134. Day and Klauder, Holder Court, Princeton University, Princeton, New Jersey, 1917–19. Gate. (Photograph: Elizabeth Moule.)

135. Collidge and Hodgdon, Weibolt Hall, University of Chicago, Chicago, Illinois, 1928. Gate. (Photograph: The University of Chicago Archives; in Jean Block, *The Uses of the Gothic: Planning and Building*, 1983.)

136. John Fisher, St. John's College, Cambridge University, Cambridge, England, 1510–16. Main gate. (Photograph: Stephen Kieran.)

137. Charles Buckridge, St. Anthony's College, Oxford University, Oxford, England, 1780. (Photograph: in Anthony Kersting and John Ashdown, *The Buildings of Oxford*, 1980.)

138. Robert Smythson, Design, probably for a Hall Screen, Nottinghamshire, England, 1586. (Photograph: Royal Institute of British Architects; in Mark Girouard, *Robert Smythson and the Elizabethan Country House*, 1983.)

139. Sebastiano Serlio, Doric Chimneypiece, woodcut from Serlio, *The Five Books of Architecture*, Venice, 1537.

140. Venturi, Rauch and Scott Brown, Presentation Board of Chimneypieces and Building Gates for Gordon Wu Hall, 1980. (Photograph: Venturi, Rauch and Scott Brown.)

141. John Akroyd and John Bentley under Warden Savile, Fellow's Quadrangle Gate, Merton College, Oxford University, Oxford, England, 1609–1610. (Photograph: in Anthony Kersting and John Ashdown, *The Buildings of Oxford*, 1980.)

142. Thomas Jackson, University Examination Schools, Oxford, England, 1882. (Photograph: in Anthony Kersting and John Ashdown, *The Buildings of Oxford*, 1980.)

143. Robert Smythson, The New Exchange in the Strand, London, England, 1609. (Photograph: Royal Institute of British Architects; in Mark Girouard, *Robert Smythson and the Elizabethan Country House*, 1983.)

144. Robert Smythson, Kirby Hall, Northamptonshire, England, 1570–73. Gable. (Photograph: National Monuments Record, Courtesy of B. T. Batsford Ltd.; in Alec Clifton Taylor, *The Pattern of English Building*, 1962.)

145. Capability Brown, Garden Pavilion, Burghley House, Northamptonshire, England, 1760. (Photograph: in Terence Davis, *The Gothick Taste*, 1975.)

146. Day and Klauder, Rockefeller College Dining Hall (formerly Madison Hall), Princeton University, Princeton, New Jersey, 1917–19. Entrance. (Photograph: Stephen Kieran.)

147. Venturi, Rauch and Scott Brown, Gordon Wu Hall, Princeton University, Princeton, New Jersey, 1980–83. Entrance. (Photograph: Stephen Kieran.)

148. Alvar Aalto, Scandinavia Bank, Helsinki, Finland, 1962. (Photograph: in Karl Fleig, ed., *Alvar Aalto Band I*, 1963.)

149. Venturi, Rauch and Scott Brown, Gordon Wu Hall, Princeton University, Princeton, New Jersey, 1980–83. Sketch of gate-entry by Robert Venturi, 1981. (Photograph: Venturi, Rauch and Scott Brown.)

150. Venturi, Rauch and Scott Brown, Gordon Wu Hall,

Princeton University, Princeton, New Jersey, 1980–83. Steel lintel over entrance. (Photograph: Stephen Kieran.)

151. Day and Klauder, Holder Hall, Princeton University, Princeton, New Jersey, 1917–19. Window. (Photograph: Stephen Kieran.)

152. Venturi, Rauch and Scott Brown, Gordon Wu Hall, Princeton University, Princeton, New Jersey, 1980–83. Door to private dining room. (Photograph: Stephen Kieran.)

153. Venturi, Rauch and Scott Brown, Gordon Wu Hall, Princeton University, Princeton, New Jersey, 1980–83. North bay window. (Photograph: Stephen Kieran.)

154. Venturi, Rauch and Scott Brown, Gordon Wu Hall, Princeton University, Princeton, New Jersey, 1980–83. South bay window. (Photograph: Stephen Kieran.)

155. Venturi, Rauch and Scott Brown, Gordon Wu Hall, Princeton University, Princeton, New Jersey, 1980–83. Longitudinal section. (Photograph: Venturi, Rauch and Scott Brown.)

156. Robert Smythson, Burton Agnes Hall, Yorkshire, England, 1601–10. (Photograph: Peter Burton; in Mark Girouard, *Robert Smythson and the Elizabethan Country House,* 1983.)

157. Edwin Lutyens, Little Thakeham, Sussex, England, 1902. (Photograph: *Country Life;* in A.S.G. Butler, *The Architecture of Sir Edwin Lutyens,* 1950.)

158. Robert Smythson, Wooton Lodge, Stratfordshire, circa 1608. (Photograph: *Country Life;* in Mark Girouard, *Robert Smythson and the Elizabethan Country House,* 1983.)

159. Venturi, Rauch and Scott Brown, Gordon Wu Hall, Princeton University, Princeton, New Jersey, 1980–83. Main stair and hall. (Photograph: Stephen Kieran.)

160. Sanderson Miller, Pomfret Castle, London, England, 1760.

Staircase. (Photograph: in Terence Davis, *The Gothick Taste,* 1975.)

161. Edwin Lutyens, Copse Hall, Upper Slaughter, Gloucester, England, 1906. Staircase. (Photograph: *Country Life;* in Terence Davis, *The Gothick Taste,* 1975.)

162. Le Corbusier, Villa Savoie, Poissy, France, 1928–30. Rail of upper ramp. (Photograph: Stephen Kieran.)

163. Venturi, Rauch and Scott Brown, Gordon Wu Hall, Princeton University, Princeton, New Jersey, 1980–83. Stainless-steel coat hooks in hall. (Photograph: Stephen Kieran.)

164. Venturi, Rauch and Scott Brown, Gordon Wu Hall, Princeton University, Princeton, New Jersey, 1980–83. Lounge with fireplace and overmantle. (Photograph: Stephen Kieran.)

165. Robert Smythson, Bolsover Castle, Derbyshire, England, 1612–14. Chimneypiece. (Photograph: Edward Piper; in Mark Girouard, *Robert Smythson and the Elizabethan Country House,* 1983.)

Preface

Peter S. Walch, University of New Mexico Art Museum

From September 3 to October 27, 1985, the University of New Mexico Art Museum hosted the exhibition, *Venturi, Rauch and Scott Brown: A Generation of Architecture.* This exhibition, organized by the Krannert Art Museum, University of Illinois at Urbana-Champaign and curated by Stephen Prokopoff, surveyed the innovative projects of two decades work from the firm and its principal in charge of architectural design, Robert Venturi.

In order to place this architecture in context, the University Art Museum invited noted architectural scholars from around the country to present papers at a symposium in Albuquerque, held October 11, 1985. We are now most pleased that the fruits of that symposium will, through this book, be made available to a wider audience.

The Albuquerque showing of the exhibition, and the symposium, were made possible in part through the generous support of the following contributors: The Friends of Art; National Endowment for the Arts; New Mexico Humanities Council; American Institute of Architects/Albuquerque Chapter; New Mexico Society of Architects; UNM School of Architecture and Planning; UNM College of Fine Arts; Antoine Predock, FAIA; Albuquerque Board of Realtors; American Business Interiors, A Division of American Furniture; Bradbury & Stamm Construction Company, Inc.; Dekker & Associates; Southwest Textbook Depository, Inc.; Sandia Federal Savings and Loan Association; Van H. Gilbert, architect.

A portion of the Museum's general operating funds for this fiscal year was provided by a General Operating Support Grant from the Institute of Museum Services, a federal agency that administers to the nation's museums.

1. Venturi and Rauch, with Cope and Lippincott, Guild House, Philadelphia, Pennsylvania, 1960–63.

2

3

2. Venturi and Rauch, Vanna Venturi House, Chestnut Hill,
Philadelphia, Pennsylvania, 1961–64.   3. Venturi and Rauch,
Trubek and Wislocki Houses, Nantucket Island, Massachusetts,
1970–71.

4. Venturi and Rauch, Brant House, Greenwich, Connecticut, 1970–73. 5. Venturi and Rauch, Best Products Showroom, Oxford Valley, Pennsylvania, 1977.

5

6. *Venturi and Rauch, Institute for Scientific Information, Phil-adelphia, Pennsylvania, 1978.*

7

7. *Venturi, Rauch and Scott Brown, Gordon Wu Hall, Princeton University, Princeton, New Jersey, 1980–83.   8. Venturi, Rauch and Scott Brown, with Payette Associates, Lewis Thomas Laboratory for Molecular Biology, Princeton University, Princeton, New Jersey, 1983–85. Facade elevation.*

8

The Architecture of Robert Venturi

1

Introduction:
The Meaning of "Both-And" in Venturi's Architecture

Christopher Mead, University of New Mexico

Since 1959, Robert Venturi has challenged the Modernist canon of orthodox architectural forms with a pluralistic affirmation of the choices offered by history. When he replaced Mies van der Rohe's aphorism, "Less is more," with his question, "Is not Main Street almost all right?"[1] he located American architecture in a broader historical, social, and physical context than had been admitted by Modernism in its utopian quest for an internationally valid style. Arguing for the "messy vitality"[2] of our built environment, Venturi has made his architecture speak on as many levels as does America's own cultural diversity. High art and popular art, classical architecture and vernacular building, picturesque regional traditions and our tradition of commercialism, all find expression in his work. This shift from a search for the singular and abstractly homogeneous solution to the study of multiple and actually heterogeneous solutions has both informed the ongoing debate over what is significant in contemporary architecture and made Venturi a symbol of the current confusion. Robert Stern's identification of Venturi as one of the "greys,"[3] as an architect of ambiguity who mediates between the exclusive "either-or" positions of black and white by exploring the hybrid possibilities of "both-and,"[4] summarizes the problem. Such an architect, and such an architecture, eludes the easy categorizations of stylistic judgment and leaves one with the awkward certainty that his work follows a coherent logic even if one cannot reduce that logic to a single solution.

Any explanation of Venturi must begin with the idea of context. Though contextualism has come to mean in the popular mind over the last twenty years little more than the hamburger stand next door, its full meaning extends beyond such literal proximity to address the larger questions of a building's place in history. For Venturi, history is not the abstraction implied by Sigfried Giedion's distinction between "constituent and transitory facts"—between a few, eternally valid principles of space and form, and the plethora of historical details whose past efflorescences have no present relevance.[5] History is seen instead as the real and necessarily complex presence of an entire past in our contemporary world, a presence shaped by the continuous evolution of those same "transitory facts" and

expressed in architecture through representational forms. A contextual reading of Venturi's architecture might first analyze the dialogue between a specific building and the specific history of its location, but it should also include the history of American architecture, the history of modern architecture, and the history of architecture in the Western world since antiquity. Contextualism is composed of multiple and overlapping references whose coherence depends upon the present action of the architect as he locates his work within the structure of history.

Venturi's view of history informs his relationship to his rhetorical nemesis, Mies van der Rohe. A revealing preoccupation with this master of reductive Modernism runs through both Venturi's architecture and his writings, yet his original critique of Mies in *Complexity and Contradiction in Architecture* (1966), usually condensed to his counteraphorism of "Less is a bore,"[6] has fostered the cliché that these two architects are irreconcilable. Judging Venturi by the very standard of "either-or" he has rejected, this cliché ignores his ability to be both for and against Mies. Because Venturi acts within the context of history, his relationship to Mies and, by extension, the Modernist tradition is inevitably more ambiguous.

The role of ornament in Venturi's architecture illustrates his practice of "both-and." In *Complexity and Contradiction*, he justified ornament as the "rhetorical element" of architecture which "enriches meaning by underscoring."[7] This belief in the rhetorical power of ornament explains the presence of both a supergraphics sign and the glazed white brick on Venturi's Fire Station #4 of 1965–67 in Columbus, Indiana (Figure 1). The white brick is particularly telling. Overlapping the lounge window at one end, climbing up the hose-drying tower and then stopping part way across the truck garage at the opposite end, this billboard willfully proclaims its formal independence from the building's interior structural reality even as it underscores the building's identity by drawing our attention to its constituent parts. Such ornament is a critique of the Modernist position codified by Henry Russell Hitchcock and Philip Johnson when they wrote in *The International Style* (1932) that the third principle of modern architecture is "the avoidance of applied ornament." Though Hitchcock and Johnson did compromise this principle by admitting both the supergraphics and the contrast of materials exploited by Venturi, they also argued for its ul-

---

1. Venturi and Rauch, Fire Station #4, Columbus, Indiana, 1965–67.

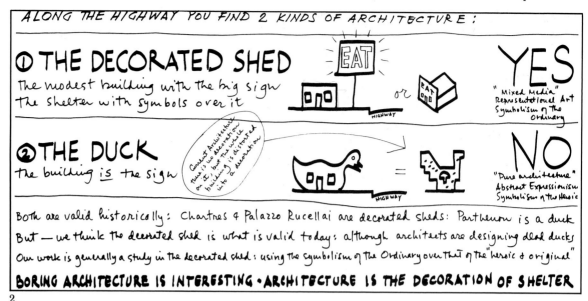

ALONG THE HIGHWAY YOU FIND 2 KINDS OF ARCHITECTURE :

① THE DECORATED SHED
The modest building with the big sign
The shelter with symbols over it

EAT   or   EAT
HIGHWAY

YES
"Mixed Media"
Representational Art
Symbolism of the
Ordinary

② THE DUCK
The building is the sign
(Commercial Architecture: there is no decoration or the whole of building is distorted into a decoration)

HIGHWAY

NO
"Pure architecture"
Abstract Expressionism
Symbolism of the Heroic

Both are valid historically: Chartres & Palazzo Rucellai are decorated sheds: Parthenon is a duck
But — we think the decorated shed is what is valid today: although architects are designing dead ducks
Our work is generally a study in the decorated shed: using the symbolism of the Ordinary over that of the "heroic & original"

BORING ARCHITECTURE IS INTERESTING • ARCHITECTURE IS THE DECORATION OF SHELTER

2

timate restriction to what might be called "structural orna-ment," which they defined as "detail actually required by structure or symbolic of the underlying structure."[8] In separating the contrasting red and white brick from either a literal or a sym-bolic correspondence to the fire station's structure, Venturi refused to accept this limitation of ornament's role.

Predictably, however, this difference between Venturian and Modernist ornament also contains its connecting similarity. In a sketch drawn in 1970 (Figure 2), Venturi and Denise Scott Brown distinguished the "Decorated Shed" from the "Duck." The decorated shed is defined as "the modest building with a big sign. The shelter with the symbol over it"; the duck is defined as "the building is the sign. [In] contemporary archi-tecture there is no decoration, but the whole building is dis-torted into a decoration."[9] By opposing the "Duck" and opting for the "Decorated Shed," Venturi and Scott Brown were doing more than rejecting the sculptural brutalism of works like Paul Rudolph's Art and Architecture Building of 1958–63 at Yale University in New Haven, Connecticut or Kallmann, McKinnell and Knowles's Boston City Hall of 1962–69 (Figure 3). They were also accepting the volumetric, box-like forms epitomized by the Modernist technology of a curtain wall stretched across a structural skeleton of steel or concrete. Their embrace of this type, despite its usual association with the aesthetics of European Modernism as communicated to an American audi-ence by Hitchcock and Johnson, was surely informed by the fact that the shed has a specifically American genealogy which dates back at least to Albert Kahn's automobile factories built early in this century.

Beginning with his commission of 1939 to design the Illinois Institute of Technology in Chicago, Illinois, Mies van der Rohe articulated this technology with single-minded clarity during the second, American half of his career. The suggested con-tinuity between Mies and Venturi can be taken a step further because Mies's Seagram Building of 1954–58 in New York City (Figure 4), its decorative bronze I-beams applied to the surface of a box, is as much a "Decorated Shed" as is, for example, Venturi's Institute for Scientific Information of 1978 in Phila-delphia, Pennsylvania (Plate 6). This filiation is confirmed by Venturi who, writing *Learning from Las Vegas* (1972) with Den-ise Scott Brown and Steven Izenour, argued that

Less may have been more, but the I-section on Mies van der Rohe's fire-resistant column, for instance, is as completely or-namental as the applied pilaster on the Renaissance pier or the incised shaft in the Gothic column. . . . Like the Renaissance vocabulary of the Classical orders, Mies's structural ornament, although specifically contradictory to the structure it adorns, rein-forces the architectural content of the building as a whole.[10]

Venturi makes several interconnected points. In the first place, it becomes clear that while Mies's I-beam might be limited to the language of structure, it nonetheless is rhetor-ical—it is an ornamental addition which, because it remains distinct from the building's real structure, can enrich meaning by underscoring. As a rhetorical element equated with the Renaissance pier, the I-beam reintegrates the Miesian box with the Renaissance palace presented a few pages earlier in *Learn-ing from Las Vegas* as "the decorated shed *par excellence.*"[11] As, however, a rhetorical element whose only reference is to the building's skeleton, the I-beam distinguishes the Modernist from the Renaissance shed, where ornament played a more generous role. In Venturi's words, "Modern architects began to make the back the front" in order to display the shed's internal structure,[12] and he goes on to note that this structural abstraction sets Mies apart from Albert Kahn: "Mies van der Rohe looked only at the backs of Albert Kahn's factories. . . . The fronts of Kahn's sheds . . . were graciously Art Deco. . . . The plastic massing up front, characteristic of this style, grandly contradicted the skeletal behind."[13] The Miesian shed with its I-beam is thus revealed, in this particularly subtle critique, to have its historical analogy in the Renaissance palace, to be consequently a historical link between the Renaissance and Venturian sheds, and yet simultaneously to be set apart from this history by its denial of the shed's facade.

If the temptation at this point is to lose patience with these ambiguities and to dismiss them as nonsense, then one has

2. Robert Venturi and Denise Scott Brown, The Duck and the Decorated Shed, *sketch diagram, 1970. 3. Kallmann, McKinnell and Knowles, City Hall, Boston, Massachusetts, 1962–69. 4. Mies van der Rohe, Seagram Building, New York, New York, 1954–58.*

3

4

failed to follow the reasoning of "both-and." Venturi explained this reasoning in an essay of 1978 whose very title is explanatory: "A Definition of Architecture as Shelter with Decoration on It, and Another Plea for a Symbolism of the Ordinary in Architecture." The essay goes on to state that "we like emphasizing shelter in architecture, thereby including function in our definition; and we like admitting symbolic rhetoric in our definition, thereby expanding the content of architecture beyond itself and freeing function to take care of itself."[14] Because shelter/function (encompassing structure as well as use) and decoration/symbolic rhetoric are both symbiotic and distinct for Venturi, he can do what Modernism could not do. Where Mies reduced the shed to its minimal, structurally abstract expression, Venturi has expanded it by turning the same shed into a discursive field for representational images drawn variously from high art, commercialism, and vernacular tradition. The Institute for Scientific Information, for example, takes the Modernist shed with its regularly gridded structure, ribbon windows, and taut skin, yet replaces the structurally symbolic I-beam with an exuberantly colored pattern of tiles which reads across the facade like some computer printout. Mies's classicizing simplicity becomes Venturi's romantic discourse between levels of meaning. In his 1978 essay, Venturi may have summarized the difference/similarity when he compared Mies van der Rohe and McDonald's hamburger stands: "A factory of Mies's is vernacular art enhanced as fine art; a McDonald's on the strip is folk art derived from fine art."[15] Mies very probably would have shuddered at this conjunction, but for Venturi this "both-and" dialogue between the recto and verso of the same architectural image is central to his work. When one sees the dialogue in Venturi's architecture between the abstractly singular form of Modernism and the actually multiple forms of history, one starts to understand his work.

The act of seeing, of looking with intelligence, is emphasized because it seems that architects and historians alike have tended to substitute passing familiarity with Venturi's architectural theory for perceptive comprehension of his buildings. The notoriety of *Complexity and Contradiction* and *Learning from Las Vegas* has obscured the simple fact that Venturi is, first of all, an architect; that, for example, his Guild House in Philadelphia was designed in 1960 (Plate 1), six years before the publication

of *Complexity and Contradiction;* that he thinks visually with forms as much as he thinks verbally with words. The interpretative bias for a philological understanding of Venturi must be balanced by a return to the expression of his ideas in architectural forms. This return provokes a series of questions: what was the substance of Venturi's education, which architects and architectural traditions have influenced his work, what are the things he has looked at, what are the forms he has chosen for his buildings, why did he choose them, and how has he composed them into a significant architecture?

The following essays by Vincent Scully, David Van Zanten, Neil Levine, Thomas Beeby, and Stephen Kieran suggest some answers to those questions. The record of a symposium sponsored by the University of New Mexico Art Museum in October 1985, these essays do not subject Venturi to a singular and consistent interpretation; each contributor—three historians and two architects—approaches Venturi with a different focus and, quite often, a different method of analysis. But if this book should therefore be read more as a collection of individual points of view than as a monograph, it does reveal an underlying and coherent conclusion. Vincent Scully, with the combined empathy and scholarship of one who has long studied Venturi, surveys Venturi's career to identify the condensation of Modernism and history that lies at the heart of his humanistic architecture. David Van Zanten, like Venturi a product of Princeton University, reconstructs the origins of its School of Architecture in order to define a pedagogical tradition whose evenhanded, eclectically tolerant, and antipolemical treatment of the history and practice of architecture explains Venturi's belief in the possibility of "both-and." Neil Levine, connecting Vincent Scully's writings and Robert Venturi's architecture, examines Venturi's work to demonstrate how he has reintegrated modern architecture with its context by replacing Modernism's abstract, exclusive, and ideal perception of history with one that is representational, inclusive, and real. Thomas Beeby, whose own work as an architect has developed from an earlier Miesian classicism to a more recent reconciliation with history, analyzes Venturi's translation, in the Trubek and Wislocki Houses, of vernacular tradition into modern architecture. Stephen Kieran, bringing to his study of Wu Hall the working knowledge of an architect who was a project manager in Venturi's office, traces the rhetorical dialogue in this building between Modernist construction and historical representation. Each essay thus reinforces the conclusion that Robert Venturi is a remarkably generous architect whose embrace of history's complexities and contradictions has inestimably enriched, but never rejected, the course of modern architecture.[16]

One last, essential point: starting with the title, this book's apparently exclusive focus on Robert Venturi must be understood inclusively to mean all the members of the firm of Venturi, Rauch and Scott Brown. The authors are keenly aware that this firm collaborates on the creation of ideas and designs, and that many of the works discussed cannot be attributed to Venturi alone. Besides the numerous assistants and project managers, there are the firm's two other principals: John Rauch, who has been a partner in the firm since 1964, and especially Denise Scott Brown, who has been a partner in the firm since 1967. The firm has had three names since 1960: Venturi and Short, 1960–64; Venturi and Rauch, 1964–80; Venturi, Rauch and Scott Brown, 1980–present.

Like Venturi's architecture, this book is the result of a collaborative effort that involves more people than those credited on the title page. Peter Walch, director of the University of New Mexico Art Museum, and Dana Asbury, an editor at the University of New Mexico Press, understood the need for this book and provided the necessary professional support. Kathy Hayden and Ron Gadbaw proved to be dedicated typists, whose patience was never exhausted by the numerous revisions of the manuscript. Among my collaborators, however, one person deserves exceptional credit: Susan Nunemaker Braun, curator of education at the University of New Mexico Art Museum. Efficient liaison between the book's contributors, Argus-eyed proofreader, and skilled obtainer of photographs, she shared with me—and solved many of—the practical problems posed by such a collaborative work. Without her, this book would not be.

Notes

1. Robert Venturi, *Complexity and Contradiction in Architecture,* with an introduction by Vincent Scully, Museum of Modern Art Papers on Architecture, no. 1 (New York: Museum of Modern Art, in association with the Graham Foundation for Advanced Studies in the Fine Arts, 1966), p. 102.

2. *Ibid.,* p. 22.

3. Robert Stern, *New Directions in American Architecture,* rev. ed. (New York: George Braziller, 1977), p. 117; this identification comes in a postscript to the original edition of 1969 in which he identified Venturi as an "inclusivist."

4. Venturi, *Complexity,* p. 23; see also pp. 30–38 on the "Phenomenon of 'Both-And' in Architecture." Venturi got the term from Cleanth Brooks, *The Well-Wrought Urn* (New York: Harcourt, Brace and World, 1947).

5. Sigfried Giedion, *Space, Time and Architecture: The Growth of a New Tradition,* 5th rev. ed. (orig. pub. 1941; Cambridge, Mass.: Harvard University Press, 1967), pp. 17–19. See the critique of this abstract perception of history in Robert Venturi, Denise Scott Brown, and Steven Izenour, *Learning from Las Vegas: The Forgotten Symbolism of Architectural Form,* rev. ed. (orig. pub. 1972 as *Learning from Las Vegas;* Cambridge, Mass.: MIT Press, 1977), p. 104.

6. Venturi, *Complexity,* pp. 24–25.

7. *Ibid.,* p. 44; this is in the context of Venturi's discussion of "the Double-Functioning Element" on pp. 38–45.

8. Henry Russell Hitchcock and Philip Johnson, *The International Style: Architecture Since 1922* (New York: W.W. Norton & Company, 1932), pp. 69–77.

9. This sketch, combining images and text, was included in the traveling exhibition, "Venturi, Rauch and Scott Brown: A Generation of Architecture," organized by the Krannert Art Museum, University of Illinois at Urbana-Champaign (1984–1986); it introduces an issue discussed at length in Venturi, *Learning from Las Vegas,* pp. 87–163 passim.

10. *Ibid.,* pp. 114–15.

11. *Ibid.,* pp. 106–7.

12. *Ibid.,* p. 114.

13. *Ibid.,* p. 135.

14. Robert Venturi, "A Definition of Architecture as Shelter with Decoration on It, and Another Plea for a Symbolism of the Ordinary in Architecture," reprinted in Robert Venturi and Denise Scott Brown, *A View from the Campidoglio: Selected Essays 1953–1984,* eds. P. Arnell, T. Bickford, and C. Bergart (New York: Harper and Row, 1984), pp. 62–67.

15. *Ibid.,* p. 65.

16. Between the symposium and the publication of this book has come Stanislaus von Moos's sympathetic study, *Venturi, Rauch & Scott Brown. Buildings and Projects* (New York: Rizzoli, 1987), D. Antal, trans.

Robert Venturi's Gentle Architecture

Vincent Scully, Yale University

Thinking about the work of Robert Venturi, and I have thought about it a good deal over the past twenty years, it struck me this time that he is a little like Franklin Roosevelt. Roosevelt saved the capitalist system in America—pretty much from itself—and was hated for it by all capitalists; Venturi saved modern architecture from itself and has been hated for it by almost all modern architects. I think the reason is this: modern architecture simply could not, would not, deal with the complexities of the city. Its urbanism, like its architecture, was abstract. So it destroyed the city, casting out everything that had been laboriously developed over the centuries to make the city worth living in.

Le Corbusier is the best example. Once he had eliminated all of traditional urbanism, which he did by the early twenties, he soon grew weary, by the early thirties at least, of the machine aesthetic with which he had replaced it. He found that he had nowhere to go except back to the primitive, the primordial—precisely because he had written out of history all of the centuries of civilized development in architecture that combine to make a city. Le Corbusier's late work embodied a primitive, sculptural force, and its proper setting could only be that of antique religion itself: the natural world. It was surely a very great, though limited, image. The High Court Building of 1951–56 at Chandigarh (Figure 5), with the continuous upward thrust of its piers, past any lintel, makes us feel empathetically the vertical stance of the soldier who stands before it. The forms are like those of a Greek temple, since both embody a challenge to the natural world. But when this primordial, primitive giant left the landscape and lumbered into our cities in the 1950s and 1960s, it laid waste to the urban landscape, flailing about with Neanderthalic roarings. Kallman, McKinnell and Knowles's Boston City Hall of 1962–69 (Figure 3) is a very good example of the late modern, so-called Brutalist buildings that despised, trampled upon, destroyed the scale of the city and, most of all, cut through the complex web of urbanistic adjustments from which a city is made.

Venturi, it seems to me, was the first to begin reversing all of that. He mitigated the abstraction of modern architecture and made it contextual once more. His buildings were prepared to get along with the other buildings in the city, to take up their roles in a gentle comedy of citizenship rather than in a

melodrama of pseudoheroic aggression. Venturi's architecture is therefore involved with healing, but it remains a modern architecture. The taut, continuous, thin wall of Gordon Wu Hall of 1980–83 at Princeton University (Plate 7), with the columnar structure visible behind the glass, creates a wholly modern gesture. It could be of no other age. Venturi shapes a contemporary architecture that is more wholly modern than that of the International Style because it can also engage in a dialogue with the architecture of the past. This seems to be the first fact about Venturi.

Another seems to be that Venturi, of all the architects I have known, has worked most through the principle of condensation. Sigmund Freud first stated this principle in the modern age when he described how what he called the "dream work" brought "dream thoughts" into "dream content." The first stage in that process was the condensation of opposites to form a "new unity." That aesthetic idea is originally Scholastic, since Scholastic philosophy employed the word *concordantia,* the reconciliation of opposites, to define what Freud meant by condensation.

We can watch Venturi work this way in his pioneering project of 1959 for a Beach House (Figure 6)—the one through which most of us became aware of his existence. He began with McKim, Mead and White's Low House of 1887 (Figure 7), which was first published by Henry Russell Hitchcock in *Rhode Island Architecture* (1939) and which had by the 1950s become a key monument in American historiography. Having written *The International Style* (1932) with Philip Johnson, Hitchcock had instinctively turned back to look at the historical alternatives to the International Style, especially the American architecture of the later nineteenth century. The Low House, with its vast, frontal gable, became the archetypal image of that way of building. For me, working on my doctoral dissertation in the late 1940s, this was the building that first engaged my interest and, indeed, launched me into a work that emerged

---

5. Le Corbusier, High Court of Justice, Chandigarh, India, 1951–56. 6. Robert Venturi, Beach House project, 1959. Model. 7. McKim, Mead and White, Low House, Bristol, Rhode Island, 1887. 8. Edwin Lutyens, Middlefield, Great Shelford, Cambridgeshire, England, 1908.

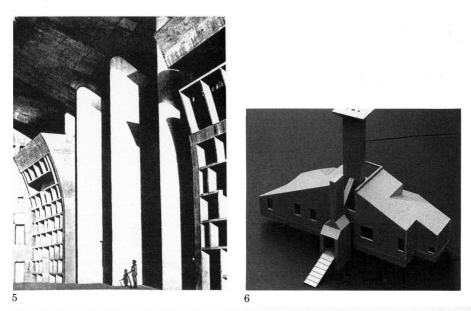

5

6

7

8

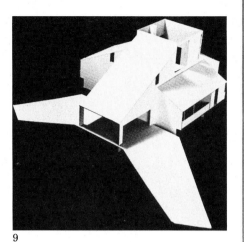

9

in part as *The Shingle Style* (1955). And it was this building that
caught Venturi's eye in 1959. He took over the frontal gable
but thrust an enormous chimney up through it. That chimney
represents a condensation of the Low House with the house
of Middlefield designed in 1908 by Sir Edwin Lutyens (Figure
8). Lutyens was without question the greatest British architect
of the early twentieth century, but he has been despised by
the Modernists because his architecture remained representational. Venturi used Lutyens to adapt the roof organization
of his project, but he blew up the chimney in scale. It is now
single and mighty, rising up behind the dunes to mark the
position of the house, confronting the sea like a medieval tower.
I remember how I resented that extravagant gesture when I
first saw the project. I said to myself: "How dare he wave that
thing in my face. Let him keep it to himself." When Charles
Moore first did his own study after Venturi's project, in his
project of 1961 for the Jenkins House (Figure 9), he ripped
out the chimney and designed the house without it.

It was Robert Stern—at that time a student of mine at Yale
University—who induced me to go look at Venturi's work. That
is the lucky thing about teaching: it provides us with young
people who force us to grow in the only way that we can grow,
by bursting the framework of preconceptions within which we
live. As we get older and our symbolic life lies more and more
inside our by now ossified previous experiences, that act of
liberation becomes increasingly difficult. It becomes harder and
harder for us to break free. Therefore, the teacher is the most
fortunate of men, so long as he allows himself to be taught,
and it is clear that a decisive conceptual transformation was
required for people of my generation to be able to appreciate
Venturi's importance.

Venturi's first important project to be built was his mother's
house, the Vanna Venturi House of 1961–64 (Plate 2 and Figure
10). Disarmingly simple after the spatial antics of late Modernism, its plan, like that of the Beach House project, is based
on a symbolic conception rather than upon one that is purely

10

*9. Charles Moore, Jenkins House project, St. Helena, Napa
Valley, California, 1961. Model.   10. Venturi and Rauch, Vanna
Venturi House, Chestnut Hill, Philadelphia, Pennsylvania, 1961–
64. Front Facade.*

11   12

spatially abstract. It is centered on the idea of the chimney, the hearth, from which—and you can feel it—the space is pulled. The space is distended from that hearth as the mass of the chimney rises up to split the house. Here the principle of condensation becomes an extremely complex and interesting one. With the chimney rising through the gable, the general *parti* derives from that of the Beach House. Now, however, the living room is half-vaulted (Figure 11), and that semicircle is picked up in the tacked-on arch of the facade; now, the whole house is rising and being split through the middle.

This conception has a distinguished genealogy. It begins with the Chandler House of 1885–86 in Tuxedo Park, New York, by Bruce Price, where a gable shelters a little, half-round Palladian window at the top and two bays on the first floor. Then, in the same year, Price built the Kent House (Figure 12)—also in Tuxedo Park—where he brought the gable around to the front and placed in it a rather larger half-round window. The facade of the Kent House is, in fact, symmetrical, but the view published in *The Builder* in 1886 makes it look as if the walled terrace were asymmetrically placed. This caught the eye of Frank Lloyd Wright when he built his own house in Oak Park in 1889 (Figure 13). Wright was, without question, the greatest American condensor of architectural opposites before Venturi; at any rate, he decisively condensed the two houses by Price—bringing them together and presenting his own "new unity," his clear Platonic triangle of frontal gable. That triangle is a pure, abstract, geometric shape, but in terms of our cultural associations, it also says "house," as a child might draw one. Wright distrusted such associations, insofar as they were historical, and soon eliminated the gable from his work.

Venturi returned to it. The associational factor itself now becomes central to Venturi's conceptual structure, endowing it with dimensions of meaning that were inaccessible to his friend, mentor, and boss, Louis I. Kahn, for whom he worked in the 1950s. Just up the road from Venturi's house for his mother is Kahn's Esherick House of 1959–61 (Figure 14), from which all associational elements that might suggest "house" have been rigorously eliminated. It is the pure abstraction of the International Style in which Kahn, in his own way, deeply believed. The building is divided into two boxes, filled with light, essentially scaleless, marvelously static. But in Venturi's

house the gable rises, opens, lifts. It is at once more sculpturally active and more like a house than are Kahn's flat-roofed boxes.

Venturi thus exploits and interweaves the two ways whereby we experience all works of art: physically and through association. They affect us empathetically, through our bodies, and associationally, through everything we know from our cultural coding. Venturi also exploits here the ancient tradition of Platonic order embodied in the essential shapes of triangle, circle, and square. The human figure fitted in the circle and the square constitutes the most obsessive image of Western architectural theory. It derives from a passage in Vitruvius, which surely has much older, probably Pythagorean, sources behind it. The circle and the square became the basis for Gothic and Renaissance architecture alike and, as ideally dematerialized by Le Corbusier, for the International Style as well. Venturi uses them as the cosmic emblem of his little house (Figure 10). He centers the square void, broken at the top, and around it he draws his circle, broken upward as well and extended by projection into the earth. The scale becomes enormous, and in the center of it all Venturi's mother sits in a kitchen chair with a pot of geraniums at her feet. The naked male hero, Leonardo da Vinci's emperor of the universe, has been superceded by a feminist image—one not shrill but wry and quiet. Aggression gives way to affection. The associational references encompass most of human history.

It can come as no surprise that Venturi has played a critical part in the liberation of women in architecture, not only in his relationship with his partner and wife, Denise Scott Brown, but in all his attitudes to women as students and as members of his staff. He has wholly abandoned the heroic, macho stance characteristic of so many architects in the recent past and has incorporated more civilized principles into the life of his firm and into his architecture.

11. Robert Venturi, Vanna Venturi House, Chestnut Hill, Philadelphia, Pennsylvania, 1961–64. Living room.   12. Bruce Price, Kent House, Tuxedo Park, New York, 1885–86. 13. Frank Lloyd Wright, Wright House, Oak Park, Illinois, 1889.   14. Louis I. Kahn, Esherick House, Chestnut Hill, Philadelphia, Pennsylvania, 1959–61.

13

14

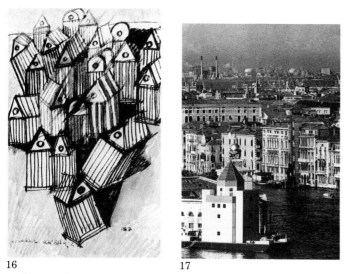

16   17

Along with that has come a larger liberation for men and women alike: a liberation from the romantic conception of the architect as the perennial inventor of the wheel. Modernism, and Late Modernism in particular, was rent to incoherence by the insistence of its practitioners upon "originality," not only because it gave rise to every kind of schizoid behavior in the concealment of sources even from the self, but also and more seriously because of the primitive assault upon the urban fabric to which the search for originality gave rise. This is the major source of the hatred with which the architectural profession fell upon Venturi: he took its most satisfying, its most childish myth away. But in doing so, Venturi profoundly rationalized and civilized the profession. Rational discourse, though rare, now became possible as it replaced the crude, shouted slogans of the recent past. Even disagreement could be imagined. When asked about some students at Princeton University who had criticized his work, Venturi said in effect, "Sure, why not. It's only architecture, not religion."

At the same time, Venturi has revived Modernism in its essential aspects. He goes back beyond the Bauhaus to the most intense moments of Modernism when it really wanted to say something, to change the world politically as in every other way. For Venturi, the political dimension is there only by analogy, but much the same excitement, the physical liveliness, the desire to communicate, is present. El Lissitzky's revolutionary poster of 1919, *Beat the Whites with the Red Wedge* (Figure 15), can be compared to Venturi's house in its use of a broken circle and its explosive, sharp-edged forms. And though Venturi did not use words in this project, as El Lissitzky does in his poster, he was soon to do so.

But, in house architecture especially, Venturi was also about to look more closely at tradition. His mother's house is very Modernist in the sense that it looks abstract, indeed like a model; Venturi abandons in it the shingles that Wright had used. In the Trubek and Wislocki Houses of 1970–71 on Nantucket Island (Plate 3), however, he turns more directly to the Shingle

Style, with which, of course, he had been deeply involved since his Beach House project. For Venturi, the two houses are also like the Greek temples at Selinus, Sicily, as they turn slightly in toward each other above the sea. Like Greek temples, they are also types—here simple, more or less transformed, vernacular types. The Wislocki House on the left is, particularly, the essence of shack and of vertical standing body. Those two qualities have similarly been appreciated by Aldo Rossi who, without contact with Venturi, has employed exactly the same shapes. In Rossi's drawing, *The Cabanas of Elba* of 1975 (Figure 16), they are like little people, active and proud, rather hectic in their competition with each other, each staring with the cyclopean eye of a circular window in its gable.

The Wislocki House is like that: we feel it standing; we sense a person. It, too, has eyes—made with the crossed mullions in the square windows. A crossed mullion prevents the window from becoming a pure void—it winks and keeps to the surface. It also has, hauntingly back in behind it somewhere, the empathetic association of the Cross itself. Rossi uses it that way with great effect in his Elementary School of 1972–76 at Fagnano Olona, and elsewhere, as in the Teatro del Mondo of 1979 (Figure 17). What a lovely little building the Teatro del Mondo is, balancing itself on its barge like a topheavy Shalako; it has all the curious innocence of a primitive type, as does the Wislocki House.

In any event, it is clear that Rossi and Venturi alike are dealing with vernacular and classical traditions in very lively ways. If we start with Wright's Hillside Home School of 1887 at Spring Green, Wisconsin, built two years before Wright's own house, we find a perfect Froebel triangle, a classical gable shape with a half-round window in it. Below the triangle is a bay, and in the bay is a big, overscaled, cross–mullion, vernacular window. This can be compared to one of Rossi's most famous architectural studies, surely done without knowledge of Wright's work, where we look through a window out on the city, with our coffee pot echoed out there in the buildings, and we see facing us Rossi's fountain of 1965 for his City Hall Square at Segrate: a little cylinder which supports a perfect triangle. The open windows employ Wright's thin, cross-axis mullions. Both Wright and Rossi use the same archetypal forms, at once vernacular and classical in their history.

15. Eleazar Lissitzky, Beat the Whites with the Red Wedge, *poster, 1919. 16. Aldo Rossi,* The Cabanas of Elba, *drawing, 1975. 17. Aldo Rossi, Teatro del Mondo, Venice, Italy, 1979. The Teatro at the Punta della Dogana, Venice.*

19

20

18

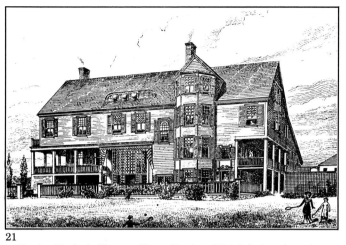

21

In the Trubek House, Venturi takes Wright's bay but chamfers only one side of it. He retains the half-round window in the gable's face but moves the vernacular window, with its cross mullions, around to the side and explodes its scale. The house does not simply "face"—it pivots and breathes. The power in all this depends upon the existence of the type itself, just as it did in Greek temples. That is how real individuality is made manifest—it can only be felt in comparison with a norm. So the Trubek and Wislocki Houses become lively animals, like the cabanas in Rossi's drawing; they are two active creatures, with porches like beaks, one thin, one fat, both about to jump as they perch above the sea.

Venturi's movement toward traditional architecture, especially toward the Shingle Style, has been very important for subsequent American work. Robert Stern was Venturi's first imitator, as he was one of his first critical supporters. In terms of artistic influence, it is interesting that Stern snuck up on Venturi from the rear when he adapted the back of the Vanna Venturi House (Figure 18) for the front of his Wiseman House of 1966–67 (Figure 19). He stretched the forms and turned the little flattened arch into a big arch and the slit in the wall into a crevasse. It is all very tormented. Stern was still trying to be original in a Late Modernist way. He was therefore trying to change his source as much as he could.

In the Mercer House of 1973 (Figure 20), Stern turned, as had Venturi, to the Shingle Style itself, specifically to a house of 1880–81 by Arthur Little, called "Shingleside" (Figure 21). This had been an important house in its time; it was published in the English *Building News* in 1882 and clearly had some effect in England upon people like C. F. A. Voysey. Stern's house may not look much like "Shingleside," but it does have its rounded bay, its porches with their high posts, and its play of the curved against the flat surface. It is all there but, oh, how deformed. Then Stern began to learn something that ar-

chitects at that time most needed to learn, which was that the closer one gets to the type, to the tradition, the stronger the building is going to be—especially where it counts: in those relationships of everything to everything else out of which the whole human settlement is made. So Stern went on to work his way back to the type, again to the Low House and to Venturi's own beginning in the Beach House project of 1959. But Stern, along with Allan Greenberg in his somewhat different way, has been much more literal than Venturi in his movement toward tradition. He has most of all tried to learn how to build and to detail in a traditional way. "God is in the details," Mies van der Rohe once said, and Stern has learned how to put it all together with those details that have always been right there in the lumber yard but which Modernist architects would not use. Stern would like to learn how to do traditional architecture without, as he says, "caricature."

But not Venturi. He is caught, right now, between the Modernists who will not forgive him and the Post-Modernists who feel that he does not go far enough. Venturi will never make a building without a comment, without something in it that can only be of now. It is not a sense of the *zeitgeist* which directs him—not a feeling of being limited by the present, but rather of being liberated by it to comment as he desires. In this, what power he has. None of the others, the literalists, has that power, but Venturi directs it always toward a contextual end.

Venturi's Coxe and Hayden Houses of 1979–82 on Block Island (Figure 22) show that. How stark they are as they look out toward the sea. One is tight and closed, but in the other, the wall of the whole bottom floor is ripped out and glazed. They are presences; they have an emotional content, special to themselves. But they are also Block Island to the life.

Having identified the gable type, Venturi obviously believed that he could do whatever he wanted with it as the context suggested. That leap of the imagination is also anti–International Style. One of the many contradictory ideas of the International Style was its conviction that there could be only one correct solution to any problem. Architecture was a matter of solutions—you solved the puzzle, like Miss Marple. Probably nothing so half-baked has ever stunted architectural thought as this conviction, or been so wholly false to the way the mind works, or to the ways in which art occurs. Nevertheless, this

18. Venturi and Rauch, Vanna Venturi House, Chestnut Hill, Philadelphia, Pennsylvania, 1961–64. Rear Facade.   19. Stern and Hagmann, Samuel Wiseman House, Montauk, New York, 1966–67.   20. Stern and Hagmann, with Alfred De Vito, Saft/ Mercer House, East Hampton, New York, 1973–75.   21. Arthur Little, "Shingleside," Swampscott, Massachusetts, 1880–81.

was the bottom line of academic criticism. That, for example, is why Michael Graves was hated so much by the "modern" architects when he won the competition of 1980 for the Portland Building in Portland, Oregon. They, like their counterparts now in New York who are attacking his proposed addition to Marcel Breuer's Whitney Museum, were annoyed by drawings in which Graves showed many different "solutions," all more or less equally valid, each absolutely different, as all works of art are different. I am sure that Graves was emboldened to do that in part by Venturi's earlier example.

On the other hand, when Venturi gets into the tension between forms, which is a consequence of working with and changing the past, he always seems to realize that he is dealing with one basic issue which, in Western civilization, and perhaps especially in America, has been the interaction between the vernacular and the classical traditions. Thomas Jefferson understood that interaction perfectly, and his buildings—like Monticello of 1768–1809—are eloquent explorations of the ways in which big, over-scaled classical elements can hold a vernacular structure, including the special demands of the program, together. From this struggle comes a wonderful vitality. When Jefferson got around to the side of Monticello (Figure 23), he did what he would not do at the front: he let windows break, gasping, through the classical entablature. In his little project for a Greek Revival house, the "Basic Tuscan Doric" from the Eclectic House Series project of 1978, Venturi says exactly the same thing (Figure 24). Here is his comment on the great American dream, a pure temple that is adjusted to ourselves. The colossal columns step forward, but little windows pop out at the side, up in the entablature, so that the rooms behind them can breathe. That tension, most eloquently embodied here, is a living one.

Venturi has sometimes been called a tool of the capitalist system by European critics, and the Brant House of 1970–73 in Greenwich, Connecticut (Plate 4), was indeed designed for a capitalist who made a lot of money out of paper. The house is very green, like new money. Venturi makes this capitalist enter through the garage, which Venturi calls "a beautiful ga-

22. Venturi, Rauch and Scott Brown, Coxe and Hayden Houses, Block Island, New York, 1979–82.

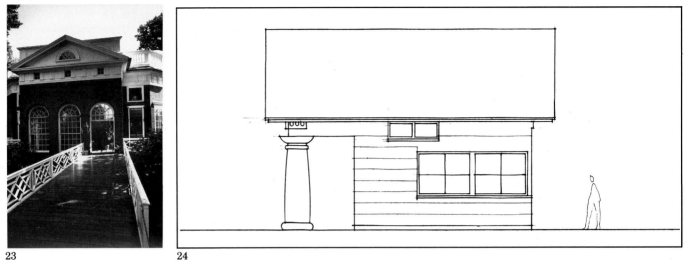

23   24

rage," to reach a beautiful formal staircase. The client did not like it very much and finally decided to expand it and not enter through the garage. So in 1977–78, Venturi prepared an addition to the house that remains one of his grandest and most sophisticated designs. A bit reminiscent of Lutyens and having the true ease of an English country house, it found no favor with the client.

The client wanted something that linked him more solidly to the great American tradition, especially the part of it that was related to horses; so he got Allan Greenberg to design a Mount Vernon on an adjoining piece of property in Greenwich. Greenberg made a very big Mount Vernon, one which is grander and heavier and more regular than the original and which has many more and richer classical details. The client made him take off the cupola; that hurt the building a good deal. Philip Johnson supported the client's desire to stand the building on a terrace—which cuts off the base of the columns from the approach and hurts the building even more.

All of this infuriated Venturi. For him, the touching and important thing about George Washington's Mount Vernon of 1740–87 was that it, like Jefferson's architecture, was all tangled up with being just a farmhouse and wanting to possess a classical stance. One problem came in wanting to center the pediment over the door, which is not quite in the center, with the result that the windows are off, as is the cupola. In his Mount Vernon project of 1979 for Greenwich (Figure 25), Venturi said, "Well, we'll center the pediment right under the cupola and center the windows under that," but then the door slides off—way off. On the other side (Figure 26), he lets the windows peek-a-boo behind the columns. And he works out a really witty plan (Figure 27) where the Palladian wings are all pulled together into a sort of ranch house. All has been changed and subverted. Venturi remains a great planner; it is the root of all his work. His design is clearly more witty than Greenberg's, and more lively. Can we say that he makes the idea of Mount Vernon more palatable, more reasonable, more fun in terms of modern life? Surely Greenberg's Mount Vernon, for all of its many solid qualities, is a rather inflated affair; Venturi's is endearing, as is the original in its own way.

In general, the comments introduced by Venturi into his buildings have a sweetness and a gentleness about them that

no other architect touches today. The Flint House of 1978 (Figure 28) stands for his work. It overlooks a cornfield. On the ground floor is a solid row of wonderfully mullioned windows, while up above a much bigger window in the gable is masked by an open arch. The arch is not arbitrary; it conceals the enormous change of scale that is taking place in the upper window. Behind the windows on the ground floor is a long, tiled room, a hall full of light. It is as simple as can be—a big farmhouse room in which, in fact, some of Venturi's own furniture would go very well. Here again Venturi has been a pioneer in the extension of modern design. His furniture, like his architecture, is simple and full of life, and it combines empathetic and associational characteristics. In his chairs, for example, Venturi combines the modern, molded plywood of Alvar Aalto with profiles and patterns that are directly reminiscent of specific period styles. Perhaps the most effective is his version of the Queen Anne Style (Figure 29), since it reflects at once the most sculptural, the most comfortable, and the most intensely American of chairs. Covered with a pattern that Venturi calls "grandmother's tablecloth," it begins to radiate the "sweetness and light" that Mark Girouard ascribed to the Queen Anne Style in his book, *Sweetness and Light. The 'Queen Anne Movement' 1860–1900* (1977).

Above the hall, lighted by the window that is masked from the outside, a music room fills the gable of the house (Figure 30). Its decoration says "music," with the wonder of a child—all cut out and painted. It is a good deal like the chairs—flat and cookie-cut and with a special, lyrical, almost childlike freshness.

The other side of the house (Figure 31) is screened by great Doric columns cut flat. Curiously enough, their unusual forms are the result of an extremely rational process. It would seem

---

23. Thomas Jefferson, Monticello, Charlottesville, Virginia, 1768–1809. South facade.   24. Robert Venturi, Basic Tuscan Doric, from the Eclectic House Series project, 1978. Side elevation. 25. Venturi and Rauch, "Mount Vernon" project, Greenwich, Connecticut, 1979. Front elevation.   26. Venturi and Rauch, "Mount Vernon" project, Greenwich, Connecticut, 1979. Rear elevation.   27. Venturi and Rauch, "Mount Vernon" project, Greenwich, Connecticut, 1979. First-floor plan.

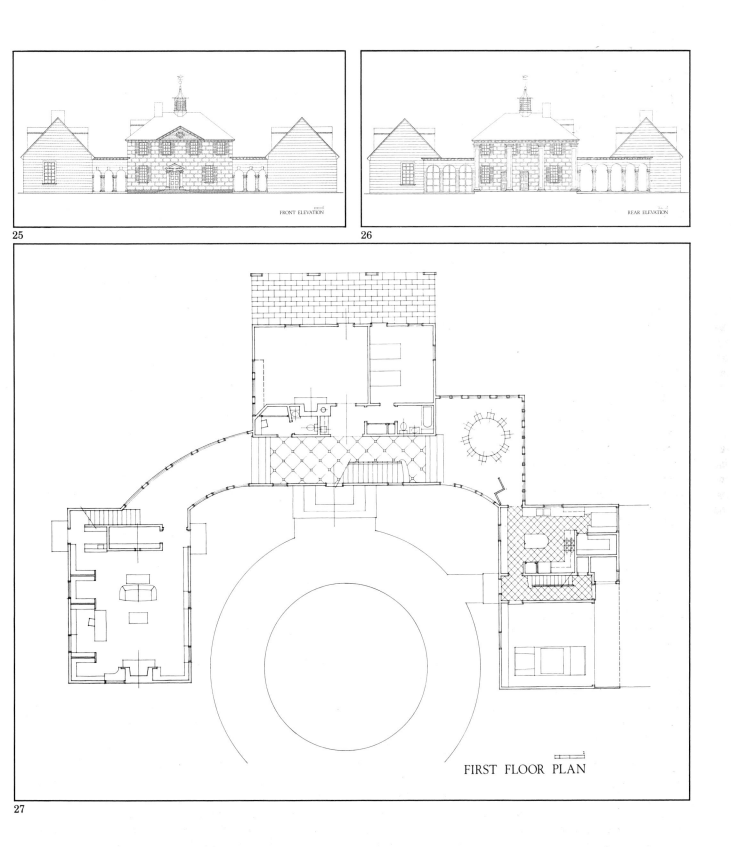

25   26

27

FIRST FLOOR PLAN

28

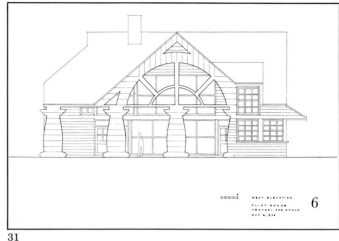

31

29

that Venturi first wanted to have big, round, Greek Revival columns. Then he changed his mind, apparently because true columns would have done two things: taken up too much space and broken up the basic unity of the house, which is that of a wall—the thin shell of the American house—that encloses a space. Moreover, by flattening the columns he could make them much broader, so that they become at once more monumental and more like a wall. They no longer fight with the containment of the house volume as a whole. This columned facade should be seen from the woods directly behind the house. The columns are seen from below as they rise up and pull out from the vernacular shell. It is Jefferson all over again: the common structure and the classical dream.

Venturi's bigger buildings are all studies in similar condensations, and they are all specifically contextual as well. We start with the Guild House of 1960–63 in Philadelphia (Plate 1), and Louis Kahn's "Brick Order." That "Order" represented a purposeful misreading by Kahn of the Roman relieving arch over its wood lintel as he had been shown it by Frank Brown at Ostia and elsewhere. Kahn turned it around to make the horizontal lintel a concrete tension member which holds the arch together. It is highly structural, very taut, very tense. Venturi adapted that "Order" in the Guild House, but he in turn misread it all in order to gesture with the brick surface past the structural frame. Venturi separated the two, and that is what makes the gesture of the surface so eloquent: we can sense its separation from the frame as it moves across the frame. Kahn's effects are structural, Venturi's dramatic.

This is the kind of difference that Kahn could never forgive in Venturi because it instantly subverts Kahn's hard-won, agonized structuralism and turns it into a gesture of humanistically conceived dramatic power. Venturi thus moves toward what the 1960s would call a "semiotic" architecture. From the beginning, he is the architect of the sign in every sense of the

28. Venturi and Rauch, Flint House, New Castle County, Delaware, 1978. East elevation. 29. Robert Venturi, Queen Anne Style Chair, 1984. 30. Venturi and Rauch, Flint House, New Castle County, Delaware, 1978. Music room. 31. Venturi and Rauch, Flint House, New Castle County, Delaware, 1978. West elevation.

word. The facade of the Guild House is pure sign since it overrides though by no means denies the structural considerations. Again, we cannot help but feel that this was the kind of thing that encouraged Graves to clad the structure of his Portland Building with a totally independent surface.

The Guild House also seems to show a knowledge of the great housing projects, especially those by Michael de Klerk, which were built in Amsterdam in the teens and twenties but which the International Style had ignored. In Michael de Klerk's Third Eigen Haard Housing Estate of 1917–20 (Figure 32), there is a big column on the street and a lower zone of a different color, like a water line, as if de Klerk were celebrating the return of the tide or suggesting a ship's plimsoll line. The complex is also like a train, with the Post Office the engine, but it invokes the ship image as well. Venturi takes the column and makes it black, and then, with the crenellated brick above, goes beyond de Klerk to the paintings of Vermeer. He invokes only a few of the innumerable connections that the human brain makes between the inexhaustible cultural items with which it is furnished. His work resonates with memory as it calls up centuries of time, including the immediate past.

El Lissitsky also reappears (Figure 15), and now Venturi's white and red planes are joined by words. How the planning authority in Philadelphia hated Venturi's sign: they wanted "Guild House" to appear in little gilt letters about the size of a brick. Venturi instead achieves a scale that is at once nobly Roman and brashly modern. He revives Modernism's passion from the days before the Bauhaus denatured it, took out the words, eliminated the exuberance, and turned it into what the Museum of Modern Art was so destructively to call "Good Design"— modern art with the sting taken out. Venturi's sign is not political but aesthetic. Nevertheless, it breaks through the gentrification of Modernism and taps the revolutionary sources of Modernism's life.

Most of all, the Guild House is a great frontal gesture, one which reminds us of other great buildings of the 1920s and 1930s, which the International Style had totally ignored. Even the Marxist critics, perhaps they in particular, had refused to honor Karl Ehn's Karl Marx Hof of 1927–28 in Vienna (Figure 33), that ultimate fortress of *Rote Wien* which fell before the assault of the right wing in 1934. Everything about it expresses solidarity, defiance, triumphal communal living. Its meaning is expressly political. Venturi had no such program to fulfill and so, instead, made an ironic gesture that invokes a painful memory. The facade of the Guild House does not rush up to lift the flags of Vienna and the Socialist Party. It rises to what Venturi called a television aerial. In fact, it was not a television aerial; that essential piece of equipment is in reality a messy little thing hidden behind the chimney. This is an abstract piece of sculpture. Everyone would have applauded if Venturi had said: "This is by the great Hungarian abstract sculptor so-and-so; it is called 'Man's Hope' and represents the triumphal union of art and architecture." But Venturi *called* it a television aerial and the critics went mad with rage. References to the old folks watching television were not regarded by them as genteel. Something about jogging would have been o.k., one supposes, or perhaps a representation of Ivan Ilyich *in extremis*. Louis Kahn told the mayor of New Haven that he would not trust an architect who put a television aerial on top of his building. He and the other critics were speaking out of the ideal stance that Modernism affected; Venturi was trying to deal with the real, and with the compassion that only irony can handle. He is wholly an artist, and his primary concern is to increase the aesthetic intensity of everyone's reaction to his building. And he did; where there might have been apathy or *pro forma* approbation, there was at least concern. The aerial was later removed and the building misses it badly, but it was part of a decade of research by Venturi into how the reaction of human beings to architecture might be intensified and enriched.

The very basis of that reaction is physical empathy turned loose to perceive the power of everyday things around us. I remember how moved I was when I first saw the Guild House, with its big, square windows. The power was there, as it is in Rossi's work. It is the power of the vernacular and the contextual—heightened and geometricized. Those windows and the brick wall and the little stringcourse all derive from the way every old building used to be built, but they are now made more conscious, stronger. "Main Street [is] almost all right,"

32. Michael de Klerk, Third Eigen Haard Housing Estate, Amsterdam, Holland, 1917–20.   33. Karl Ehn, Karl Marx Hof, Vienna, Austria, 1927–28.

32

33

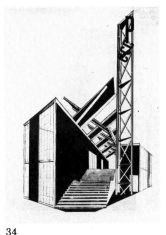

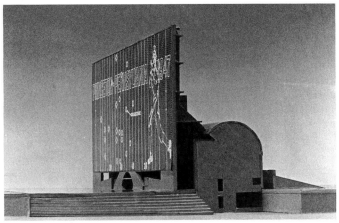

34   35

Venturi said in *Complexity and Contradiction in Architecture* (1966). "Almost." It can be made better, yet it is a viable architectural structure that is not to be outraged or destroyed. Louis Kahn, by contrast, inhabited an ideal world. His buildings on the Indian subcontinent, his Government Center of Bangladesh in Dacca, Pakistan, begun in 1962, are perfect in this regard. There they are, timeless, scaleless, structural beings of wonderful silence, with a monumentality that transcends function or place. But Venturi's rather similar forms stand right there on the street. Clarified and ennobled, they signify the presence of dignified human beings in the American mainstream.

The most intense and enduring hatred toward Venturi developed when he wrote, with Denise Scott Brown and Steven Izenour, *Learning from Las Vegas* (1972) and designed his architecture of the signboard: an architecture to attract our attention from our automobiles, an architecture to be seen from the fast-moving street. Critics like Kenneth Frampton, who has a deep and obsessive dislike of Venturi, called this kind of architecture "cynical populism." For Frampton, populism means, basically, American. It also means something not of the European avant-garde; something vulgar, which somehow plays into the hands of American capitalism by imitating the signs of the strip.

Venturi is neither populist nor cynic. The facade of his Fire Station #4 of 1965–67 (Figure 1), for example, when compared with the signs of Las Vegas, is not at all like them. It is abstracted and clarified: it is modern architecture strengthening something "almost all right." It is modern architecture that, like Konstantin Melnikov's constructivist Soviet Pavilion of 1924–25 (Figure 34), wants to project information, to shout that this is the mighty Engine Number 4, which is ready to explode through the doorway to do battle with the flames. The white brick of the Fire Station cuts across the functional areas (the windows of which are all different according to the needs of the rooms) to rush up to the big number 4, grand in scale and triumphantly projected. Frampton has nothing against the Soviet Pavilion; why should he be against this? There is nothing cynical or even capitalist about a fire station. In fact, Venturi's building was designed well before he did his study of Las Vegas. That research came after he had perceived its possibilities

through works like this.

Venturi's most important project in this regard may well be his project of 1967 for the Football Hall of Fame, which he called a "Billding Board" (Figure 35). The automobiles were intended to drive up and park in great waves. In front of them, beyond a wonderfully classic *parterre d'eau*, Venturi raised the great billboard facade, which would electronically and rather improbably show Princeton beating Pennsylvania. Behind it, reached through a low, spreading arch at the base of this semiotic marvel, were the exhibition halls (Figure 36) where, among other things, lasers would conjure up figures out of thin air, three-dimensional images hurtling through space. There can be little doubt that the art of illusion, the art of the television screen and of electronic fantasy, will play a considerable role in the architecture of the future, much as painting and sculpture did in the architecture of the past. In any case, Venturi's billboard became the model for what Piano and Rogers intended to build at the Pompidou Center in Paris (1977). They hoped to complete the building with a great electronic screen, like Venturi's, but it was cut out of the budget. It could only have added to the wonderful vitality of the plaza in front of it, and might have proved more durable than the exposed science-fiction structure of the building, which now seems to be well on the way to falling apart.

Venturi's project of 1969 for the Thousand Oaks Civic Center in California (Figure 37), a competition he did not win, is also a vast sign. One first glimpses it from afar on the freeway; coming closer but still far away, one sees that it says "THOUSAND OAKS" at a great scale. A colossal American flag, supported on the famous false front of the American western town, crowns the complex. Venturi clearly understands how we see things on the American freeway, in American space. Closer yet (Figure 38), the sign says "SAND OAK" and looms overhead.

34. Konstantin Melnikov, Soviet Pavilion, International Exposition of the Decorative Arts, Paris, France, 1924–25. Presentation drawing.   35. Venturi and Rauch, Football Hall of Fame project, Rutgers University, New Brunswick, New Jersey, 1967. Model.   36. Venturi and Rauch, Football Hall of Fame project, Rutgers University, New Brunswick, New Jersey, 1967. Interior perspective.

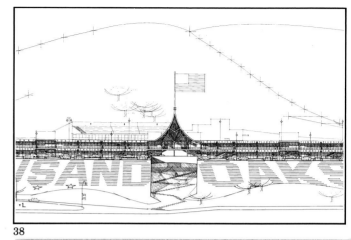

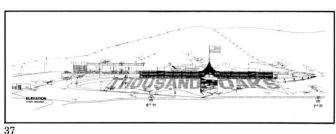

37

38

One cannot talk properly about Venturi without spending a good deal of time on things he was never able to build, competitions he did not win. The Franklin D. Roosevelt Memorial project of 1960 for Washington, D.C., was one of the first—a superb landscape space. Then, much later in his career, the Westway Development project of 1980–84 for New York City (I never thought I'd be rooting for a throughway)—a noble urban park. Or the Brighton Beach Housing competition of 1968 for Brooklyn, New York (Figure 39), where he projected a splendid series of apartments, all of which had a view of the water—as did the old apartments on the street behind the project. The winning entry by Wells and Koetter was a pastiche after Le Corbusier, Kahn, and Giurgola. It blocked everybody's view with tormented shapes and finally could not be built. But the jury was profoundly swayed by Philip Johnson's negative opinion, when he said, in effect: "Why, Venturi's project looks like any old apartment building you see around New York." Two years later, when he wanted to build on Welfare Island, Johnson had decided that "I want my building to look like any old building around New York," because, being quick on the uptake, he had come to know by that time what the score really was.

Or again, Venturi's Transportation Square office building project of 1967 (Figures 40, 41), was blocked by the Washington Fine Arts Commission, headed by Gordon Bunshaft, after it had won first prize in the competition. The important building in that project was, of course, the big one with the dome on it at the end of Maryland Avenue, and there was also a preexisting office building across the street. Venturi's building responded to those two buildings, at once complementing its neighbor and directing attention down the avenue toward the Capitol. Behind

39

37. Venturi and Rauch, Thousand Oaks Civic Center project, Thousand Oaks, California, 1969. Elevation.   38. Venturi and Rauch, Thousand Oaks Civic Center project, Thousand Oaks, California, 1969. Detail elevation.   39. Venturi and Rauch, Brighton Beach Housing project, Brooklyn, New York, 1968. Model.   40. Venturi and Rauch, with Caudill, Rowlett and Scott, Transportation Square project, Washington, D.C., 1967. View toward Capitol; view east along Interior Way.   41. Venturi and Rauch, with Caudill, Rowlett and Scott, Transportation Square project, Washington, D.C., 1967. Site plan.

40

41

42

43

44

its front plane, a lively shopping street was to have been concealed—Main Street brought into context. The commission refused to approve the design. Venturi cited Alvar Aalto as a precedent, and the setback of his design is in fact a lot like Aalto's National Pensions Institution Building of 1952–56 in Helsinki, Finland (Figure 42). Bunshaft reportedly said: "It's an insult that you should mention Alvar Aalto's name, Venturi. You're not worthy to mention Alvar Aalto's name in this context. What we're gonna have here is a building that stands in the center of space with space all around it." So Venturi, to save the developer's money, designed what Bunshaft demanded, but he kidded him a little, maybe, by giving him a pattern on the pavement that was the same as the pattern on the building. Bunshaft's committee did not like that either. Finally, Venturi came in with one they would accept—each project, of course, somewhat less good than the first—but it was too late to build it and the developer had to withdraw for financial reasons; here was another project that Venturi did not get.

Another example is the Mathematics Building project of 1969 for Yale University (Figure 43), with which Venturi won an enormous competition as the unanimous choice of a large and varied jury led by Kevin Roche. This, too, was a contextual triumph on its street. Opening like a great gate up Prospect Street, it would have looked up the hill toward the science complex on the summit and marked the entrance to the humanities below. The building is shaped in a wonderful, gentle curve, very simple and strong, with the library marked by a monumental cross-mullioned window that opens generously up the street. Venturi won, but then the donor died, the building costs rose, and it was never built.

These disappointments make it especially appropriate that Venturi's alma mater backs him so strongly now. The president of Princeton University has become his most enthusiastic supporter since he built Gordon Wu Hall (Plate 7). I have since

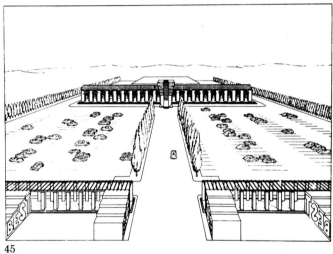

45

42. Alvar Aalto, National Pensions Institution Building, Helsinki, Finland, 1952–56. 43. Venturi and Rauch, Mathematics Building project, Yale University, New Haven, Connecticut, 1969. Perspective. 44. Robert Stern, Best Products Showroom project, 1979. Model. 45. Michael Graves, Best Products Showroom project, 1979. Perspective.

been saddened by Robert Stern's negative remarks about this building. He calls it "sly" (in a strange television series called "Pride of Place") when it is in fact strong and decisive, splendid with its older Tudor neighbors, and powerful in its commentary on the relationship between skeletal and bearing-wall forms. The stretch of surface, the expansion joints brought down through phantom keystones which are themselves spread non-structurally across the wall, all emphasize the dynamic tensions which can be felt to exist in a cladding wall that must, for fundamental architectural reasons, play a civic and intelligent role in a university's special kind of urban context. The abstracted Tudor gateway further emphasizes those relationships. Here is Venturi's inveterate contextuality, foreign to the egos of most architects: the preexisting buildings on the site shape his, which then improves them.

Venturi has often lost projects for the very worst of all reasons—for P R reasons. He does not sell himself as well as many architects do. When it comes to the sharkskin-suited phase, with the illuminated models, he really is an anti-hero and just cannot do it. He comes across as being too off-hand, as if he were not trying hard enough. It is really a question of taste and propriety. When, for example, the Best Products competition to decorate its outlets on the Strip came up, Venturi was not in the competition. But he had, in 1977, designed

47

46

one of the buildings, for Oxford Valley, Pennsylvania (Plate 5). All he did was put a kind of flowered wall paper on it. I remember one of those noncritics in one of those awful pseudo-European periodicals saying, in effect: "Here's an example of a great opportunity lost. Venturi might have done something like the others, like Stern and Graves, and he just didn't rise to the occasion." The others rose all right. Robert Stern did a project (Figure 44) with which I should be pleased because he called it "The Earth, the Temple and the Goods." But still, the mind asks: "Why all those scary columns, that Sicilian pediment? It's only Best Products, after all." Michael Graves produced a vast stoa (Figure 45), with solemn columns enclosing a majestic forum. Again the mind asks why. What these projects lack is the old classical virtue of decorum, of propriety. The program simply could not support such whoop-de-do without embarrassment. It is ridiculous to try to turn Best Products into a monstrous temple or a colonnaded garden. All you can properly do is wallpaper it. And how beautiful Venturi's building is, how the pattern so easily takes off, far beyond Stern's gestures, to rise out of the earth and slide up to the sky. Its virtues are in the end classical ones.

The same is true for a computer building, Venturi's Institute for Scientific Information of 1978 in Philadelphia (Plate 6). The facade, seen alone, looks like a computer printout, as if Venturi were being either cute or too off-hand. But when seen in the context of its street, which is made up of long, modernist horizontals, the facade enriches the whole environment of the street and enforces its intrinsic order—and it does so without trying to be anything it really is not. It is another act of propriety. Venturi knows beyond all else when to hold back. Almost no other living architect has the perception, or the modesty, to be able to do that. And here the context was International Style.

Most architects today design only surfaces; it is a tradition that goes back to Louis Sullivan's skyscrapers. One of Venturi's surfaces is on the Lewis Thomas Laboratory for Molecular Biology of 1983–85 at Princeton University (Plate 8). The first reaction of everyone who has seen it is to hate it. This is the building which aroused the distaste of the Princeton students to whom I referred earlier. Here is an architect who is still able to shock us after all these years, who pushes our perceptions to the limit so that we almost always pull back at first. (Nothing attests more to Venturi's unerring instinct for life than this.) Look at how dense that surface is, how passionately dense as Venturi keeps the mullioned windows small, almost solid. Then he stretches a fat, round ogive over the entrance without any supporting column. This has guts to it. Everything that is strong will always, like the outrageous chimney of the Beach House project, make us angry at first. We have to protect our little worlds, do we not?

I have been hard on the International Style in this talk, but Venturi's project of 1981 for the Khulafa Street Building in Baghdad (Figure 46) is in the International Style, a building to be built out of cast-in-place concrete with just a little lacy stuff to make it Islamic. It is pretty good and could shape a good Iraqi street. In fact, the president of Iraq loved Venturi's work, and if the war with Iran had not intervened, a good deal of it would probably have been built. Venturi's astonishing project of 1983 for the State Mosque in Baghdad was the major casualty. Though it did not win the competition, it was liked best by the president. There is a most astoundingly brave gesture on the inside (Figure 47), where the infinity of God is carried on vast beams made up of open and visually weightless arches—below the springing of those arches, all the columns have been removed. It is as "modern" as the reaction of the Bauhaus designer who wanted to span the Johnson Wax Building with a single beam—except that in Venturi's mosque every column is somehow present, a ghostly company miraculously phantomized. At the same time, there is gentleness everywhere. All the surfaces are decorated and show care, even love. This is the commodity with which Venturi deals. For a man who has rejected heroic pretensions and turned architects toward a more civil role, Venturi is surprisingly complete. From his chairs to his mosque, from the Guild House to the Trubek and Wislocki Houses and Gordon Wu Hall, not to mention Times Square and Westway, Venturi touches the core of modesty and intelligence in all of us and endows the rather frightening monster of modern America with a curious sweetness of heart.

---

46. *Venturi, Rauch and Scott Brown, Khulafa Street Building project, Baghdad, Iraq, 1981. Model. 47. Venturi, Rauch and Scott Brown, State Mosque project, Baghdad, Iraq, 1983. Interior perspective.*

The "Princeton System" and the Founding of the School of Architecture, 1915-20[1]

David Van Zanten, Northwestern University

To David Coffin, upon his retirement

In 1921, the foundation was laid at Princeton for McCormick Hall to house the Department of Art and Archaeology in its northern half and the newly established School of Architecture in its southern half, with a large cast room and an art historical library in the middle (Figure 48). The structure was the embodiment of the ideas of two remarkable men: Allan Marquand and Howard Crosby Butler. Marquand (1853–1924)—the son of the New York banker, Henry Marquand, trained at Princeton, Union Theological Seminary, the University of Berlin, and Johns Hopkins—was the founder of the Princeton Department of Art and Archaeology in 1883 and the animus of what had become a sophisticated American program in the history and theory of art.[2] Butler (1872–1922) had been a brilliant product of the department in the 1890s and had gone on to become a charismatic teacher and celebrated explorer and archaeologist as well as the founder and director of the Princeton School of Architecture.[3] The building had been paid for by Cyrus McCormick, the wealthy Chicago reaper manufacturer, a graduate of Princeton and the father of Gordon McCormick, one of the first products of Butler's program who was then about to join him at his excavations at Sardis in the summer of 1922.

The institution and the building projected to house it were unique ones. The Princeton School of Architecture was the only one in the United States to be thoroughly integrated with a program in art history and archaeology and to be directed by a historian rather than a professional designer.[4] The building it shared with the Department of Art and Archaeology, rising high in the middle of the low, spreading, Collegiate Gothic Princeton campus, was Italianate in style and stuccoed in red and yellow in contrast to the grey, green, and purple of the surrounding fieldstone dormitories. It was all the more remarkable for being designed by the unbending Gothicist (who was also the University Architect), Ralph Adams Cram, but it seems to have been meant to symbolize a compromise between the classical tradition of art and the medieval nuances of Anglo-Saxon culture.[5]

When the building was dedicated on June 16, 1923, it was an empty shell. Butler had died suddenly in Paris on August 12, 1922. Marquand, called back to the chairmanship he had finally relinquished in May 1922, was soon to die himself, on September 24, 1924. The faculty that they had gathered for the architecture school project were despondent.[6] Yet the shell itself—not just the building, but also the system of instruction that Butler, in cooperation with Marquand, had conceived—survived and was carried on by Butler's staff: the designer, Sherley Warner Morgan, together with the historian, Earl Baldwin Smith. They, in turn, trained a generation of men who carried on the system down to Morgan's retirement as director in 1954 and beyond: Richard Stillwell, George Forsyth, and Donald Drew Egbert. The "Princeton System," with its integration of architectural design, history, and archaeology, in the end became a significant force in American architecture, even if only as a projection of Butler's original conceptions.

Robert Venturi was a product of this school. He studied in it as an undergraduate architect in 1944–47 when the program was still a "section" of the Department of Art and Archaeology (chaired, in those years, by E. B. Smith). From 1947 to 1950 he advanced through the graduate School of Architecture, then directed by Morgan. Today one thinks of him alongside Charles Moore, who was a graduate architect in the program (1954–57) just after Morgan's resignation (as well as a researcher and instructor in 1957–59),[7] and Michael Graves, who has taught in the school from 1961. Yet Venturi came first, and he received the experience to its fullest extent. If Butler was the school's creator, Venturi was its final justifying product.

I

There are two forces in this story: Butler and Princeton. Howard Crosby Butler was an energetic and romantic figure; Princeton a profoundly traditional institution which, once set moving in some direction by men like Marquand and Butler, might proceed forward with insuperable momentum. The result, in the case of the Princeton School of Architecture, was a brilliant if quirky idea laid down swiftly by Butler in 1915–22, then adhered to with remarkable consistency by his students for the next half-century.

Butler's friend, William Dix, called him "Princeton's T. E.

---

48. *Ralph Adams Cram, McCormick Hall, Princeton University, Princeton, New Jersey, 1917–23.*

48

Lawrence." The description is apt not just because Butler rode about the Syrian Desert, but more important because he was an intensely committed, unmarried man who organized others to undertake exotic enterprises.[8] Born in Croton Falls, New York, in rural Westchester, he earned bachelor's and master's degrees at Princeton in 1892 and 1893. Between 1893 and 1897 he was "Fellow in Archaeology" in Marquand's department while also studying architecture at Columbia. In 1897–98 he was a Fellow at the recently established American School of Classical Studies in Rome. This was preparatory to his first great project: the architectural and photographic survey of the abandoned late Roman and Early Christian cities in the Syrian Desert, which he carried out in 1899–1900. He returned for two further surveys in 1904–5 and 1909. Meanwhile he taught in the Department of Art and Archaeology during the academic years 1895–96 and 1896–97 and published two popular books, *Scotland's Ruined Abbeys* (1899) and *The Story of Athens* (1902).

Beginning in 1902 he became a regular member of the department, but he taught courses that involved drawing exercises and that eventually would evolve into the architecture program.[9] In 1905 he became the first Resident Master of the Graduate School, established in that year by Dean Andrew West in a private house near the university. He remained in that capacity during the rest of his life, aiding West with the planning and erection of Ralph Adams Cram's celebrated Graduate College in 1909–13. Simultaneously he embarked on his most spectacular archaeological enterprise, the excavation of ancient Sardis, inland from Izmir in Turkey. The famous Temple of Artemis there had been buried by landslides up to the necking of its columns, but by raising large sums from New York backers (especially J. Pierpont Morgan) Butler mounted a massive digging operation in 1910, 1911, 1912, and 1913 that laid it bare. He brought back a whole column's base, capital, and part of its shaft that henceforth has terminated the southern cross-axis of the Metropolitan Museum of Art (Figure 49).

Turkey's involvement in World War I forced Butler to suspend the Sardis excavation in 1914, but his tremendous energy immediately flowed in another direction: the founding of a

---

49. Installation of fragments of the Order of the Temple of Artemis at Sardis in the Metropolitan Museum of Art, New York.

professional architecture program at Princeton. In 1915 the department hired Butler's old student, Sherley Warner Morgan, then pursuing an architectural degree at Columbia, to teach a course entitled "Architectural Drawing." In 1916–17 the catalogue listed him teaching a more advanced course, "Allied Elements," which seems to have been the first departmental course in creative architectural design.[10] At the same time the Princeton Architectural Association was founded with Butler and Morgan at its head. This was an organization of interested students concerned initially with agitation for an architecture building, succeeding sufficiently that $100,000 was in hand and Cram's designs for McCormick Hall complete by the end of 1917.

The war intervened again at this moment, with America's entry into the conflict and Morgan departing for service, but in 1920 Princeton's first M.F.A. in architecture was awarded to Robert Barnard O'Connor. In the fall of that same year the School of Architecture finally and officially appeared in the university catalogue, with Butler as its director, Morgan as its secretary, and a faculty consisting almost exclusively of the Art and Archaeology faculty. By the end of that academic year construction was begun on McCormick Hall, and in the summer of the next year Butler returned to Sardis to survey the possibility of reopening his excavations. On his return from that trip he was stricken in Paris and died.

Princeton was a force in this story equal to Butler because of its tendency to self-perpetuation. This had not been especially characteristic of the Department of Art and Archaeology. With the exception of Marquand and Butler, all of the early faculty members had been trained elsewhere, especially at the pioneering graduate university, Johns Hopkins: Arthur Frothingham (hired 1886, from Hopkins), Oliver Tonks (1905, replacing Frothingham, from Harvard), Charles Morey (1906, from the University of Michigan and the American Academy at Rome), Frank Jewett Mather (1910, from Hopkins), and George Wicker Elderkin (1911, replacing Tonks, from Hopkins). But in the case of the architectural section, the case was different. Butler himself set the model. He, in turn, brought in Sherley Warner Morgan, Clarence Ward, and Earl Baldwin Smith. Morgan's early career we have just summarized. He succeeded Clarence Ward, who was A.B. and A.M. from Princeton in

1905 and 1906 and Butler's assistant from 1910 to 1915, when he accepted a post at Oberlin. Smith came to Princeton from Bowdoin in 1911 and, after studying with Butler, became his closest assistant and, in 1922, his literary executor.[11] After Butler's death in 1922, Morgan and Smith dominated the program and hired three young architect-historians who had passed from the School of Architecture to the Department of Art and Archaeology doctoral program: Richard Stillwell, 1925; George Forsyth, 1927; Donald Egbert, 1929. With them Morgan hired a design instructor from the Architecture School, Francis Comstock (B.A. 1919, M.F.A. 1923). In 1928 there was only one important outsider in the program: the French chief design critic, Jean Labatut. He had brought no French assistants with him, however, and never served as director.

II

There were two things that, at first glance, distinguish Butler's conception of the Princeton School of Architecture: the emphasis given to history courses in the curriculum and the lack of a chief design critic.

Demonstrating the first point is the schedule of courses worked out between Butler and Marquand at the inception of the architecture program in which four history courses were required in both the junior and senior years of the bachelor's program and two history courses during the first graduate year:

Junior Year: History of Architecture (ancient and medieval), Ancient Art, Medieval Art.

Senior Year: History of Architecture (Renaissance and modern), History of Ornament (two terms), Italian Sculpture.

First Graduate Year: Italian Painting, Northern Painting.[12]

That is, the student was required to take the entire basic offerings of the department of Art and Archaeology in architectural history plus the three "classic" courses in figurative art: Italian Renaissance sculpture, Italian Renaissance painting, and Flemish painting. In Venturi's day, during the 1940s, this curriculum was still essentially in effect, except that the history of ornament had been dropped from the undergraduate sequence and the figurative art courses of the first graduate year

had become Renaissance and Modern sculpture and Modern painting. Not only that, the content of the courses would seem to have been much the same because of the Princeton tradition that course material was a departmental affair and did not vary fundamentally regardless of who taught it. The archaeologist Stillwell, for example, taught Venturi's Renaissance architecture course. Significantly, the history professors were listed as members of both the Department of Art and Archaeology and the School of Architecture. In the 1920–21 catalogue, Marquand, Butler, Mather, Morey, Elderkin, and Smith were all included. Indeed, the only design instructors on that faculty were Morgan, "Assistant Professor of Architecture," William Woodburn Potter, "Lecturer on Architecture," and Edwin Avery Park, "Instructor in Architecture" (part-time), the three lowest men in the academic hierarchy and thus the least influential in the administration of the program. Furthermore, into the 1950s the undergraduate architectural program was a "section" of the Department of Art and Archaeology, although always headed by Sherley Warner Morgan.

The reasons for this integration of the history and design courses are stated in the university catalogue of 1920–21:

Its curriculum is based on the belief that an architect should have a well-rounded education in liberal studies, that he should understand and appreciate the other arts in their relation to architecture, and that he should be taught the science of building construction as a part of his training in design, rather than as an art in itself.

The catalogue goes on to explain the lack of a chief designer:

In contrast to the usual plan of having one prominent critic of design, necessarily an adherent of a single style and method, the Princeton system offers the student the advantage of coming into contact with several points of view, and of receiving his theoretical training from a group of men, each of whom is eminent in one of the several fields of modern architectural design.

The advisors were to write up the design programs and criticize the results "in personal interviews with the students."

This was basically the Beaux-Arts system in Paris where

50

the students themselves organized a theoretically endless number of ateliers by presenting themselves to professional architects whom they wished to have as masters.[13] But in the case of Princeton, the *maîtres d'ateliers* were selected by Butler himself and represented a cross-section of the profession. In this first list there were the Graeco-Roman Classicists (Chester Holmes Aldrich, Henry Bacon, S. B. P. Trowbridge), the Gothicists (Ralph Adams Cram, Charles Z. Klauder, C. Grant LaFarge) and the eclectic Beaux-Arts men (Thomas Hastings, Lloyd Warren). It was intended that a different one of these men would serve as the principal design critic during each of the three terms into which the year was then divided. As time passed incipient Modernists of various hues were added: Harvey Wiley Corbett, Raymond Hood (both appearing first in the 1923–24 catalogue), Eric Gugler (1925–26), Arthur Loomis Harmon, George Howe (both 1927–28), and Ralph Walker (1928–29).

The question is: how did this work? We glimpse the problem of this question in several letters Earl Baldwin Smith wrote Marquand immediately after Butler's death in 1922. On September 9, 1922, he wrote:

We must realize that at any time the present system of design instruction may break down. It has been a big success to date, but that success has been wholly due to Mr. Butler's personal ability to get the big architects interested and willing to take the task of coming down seriously. The second they begin to treat it lightly, as they did at Columbia, we will have to get a very big man in design, paying him probably ten thousand, if we are going to compete with the other schools.[14]

Smith notes the difficulty of getting another historian to head the program, "who will bring us prestige, scholarship, a knowledge of practical architecture fitting him to run the school, and an ability and willingness to give four courses a term." But he is equally unhappy about hiring a "big architect" because if it did not work, "we [would] have an expensive full-time professor with the necessity of getting another in design." Smith is firmly against any doctrinaire design instructors, writing on August 29 of the possibility of hiring Lloyd Warren (Whitney Warren's brother and partner):

. . . I am not sure of my judgement. At first he made a big impression on me. Certainly he has done a fine work in New York [Grand Central Station]. On the other hand the young architects did not like his instruction; he is a man devoted to the Beaux Arts ideal and himself an advocate of Louis XVth style. In my talks with him I found his knowledge surprisingly superficial outside of French architecture and very dogmatic. It should be added that he is a fine organizer; but would there not be a danger of his organizing the School of Mr. Butler's creation into a little Beaux Arts atelier?[15]

He preferred the candidacy of the more eclectic Grant LaFarge, the original architect of St. John the Divine in New York.

In trying to put things together again, Smith and Morgan invited three designers to take charge during the year 1922–23—Frederick A. Godley, Henry Bacon, and S. B. P. Trowbridge—following plans already agreed upon with Butler.

Butler's and Morgan's efforts to avoid clear stylistic commitment in formulating their program makes one curious about their own architectural endeavors. Butler was an excellent draftsman,[16] had some professional training, and, as we have seen, was important in the erection of Cram's Graduate College and McCormick Hall. He is also credited with several original designs: the eating club, Tiger Inn (1895), which he had helped found;[17] a temporary arch (on the lines of that at Benevento) erected for the university's sesquicentennial celebration in 1896; and his childhood parish church in Croton Falls[18] in 1899 (Figure 50).[19] One might have expected a firm commitment to archaeological classicism in Butler's interventions and designs but, in fact, with the exception of the ceremonial arch, they are all medieval in style. Princeton had been the site of the most impressive demonstration of the American Collegiate Gothic style, beginning with Cope and Stewardson's Blair Arch of 1896, continuing with Woodrow Wilson's development of the campus during his presidency in 1901–9, and culminating with the appointment of Ralph Adams Cram as the university architect in 1907.[20] Butler seems to have supported this development heartily because of its expression of the English origins

50. Howard Crosby Butler, Presbyterian Church, Croton Falls, New York, 1899.

of American culture and education.[21] More important, however, each one of the designs Butler was involved with appears to be a specific and logical solution to local circumstances. The Graduate College was to create a monastic environment for graduate study and appropriately follows an English collegiate pattern.[22] McCormick Hall was in a difficult, central campus location, and we have already quoted Butler's explanation of the adoption of an Italianate style for it. Tiger Inn was an undergraduate club and is a caricature of a Tudor inn, in the manner of the contemporaneous Hasty Pudding clubhouse at Harvard designed by the most serious architect Wheelwright. The Croton Falls church is an American country chapel of wood, covered with cedar shingles, with some Gothic tracery to suggest its ecclesiastical nature. Butler thus seems not to have been trying to establish any single architectural vocabulary but instead to adopt the most appropriate solutions from those already evolved by the profession.

Morgan, though a professional architect, was similar in his attitude. During the 1920s he was responsible for three large designs: a faculty housing group near the railroad station (1921, with Park, Figures 51, 52), the Antioch Court and back wing of McCormick Hall (1927), and Westminster Choir College nearby in Princeton. Each is in a different style but each responds carefully to its specific situation. The faculty housing, in a particularly reticent and domestic stuccoed English medieval style, seems the quintessential Princeton habitation complex under its spreading trees. The McCormick Hall addition is Italian Gothic trying to be like what Cram would have done himself to extend the building, with certain simplifications. Westminster Choir College is red brick Colonial, adopting another, simpler (and cheaper) type of American traditional imagery often used for small institutional complexes. The point is less the style chosen than its immediate propriety and the care taken in execution.

III

The necessity of a lead designer could not, however, be avoided. Already upon Butler's death Mather had suggested getting E. Raymond Bossange, a Columbia-trained architect and the director of the College of Fine Arts at Carnegie Institute in Pittsburgh. He was hired as Professor and Director of the School of Architecture in the spring of 1923.[23]

For some reason Bossange was not a success, resigning in 1926 to become the director of the School of Fine Arts at New York University from that year until his death in 1947. He was replaced by Frederick d'Amato, an Italian-born Beaux-Arts product (student of Victor Laloux), who had worked for Edward Bennett in Chicago around 1912 and was currently engaged as an urban planner and design teacher in Paris.[24] D'Amato was only a lecturer, then an associate professor, the same as Morgan who had been promoted in 1925. D'Amato was well received, but on October 1, 1927, after only a year of teaching, he died.

D'Amato's successor was Jean Labatut, taking up his duties in the fall of 1928 as "Critic in Architectural Design" (listed behind Smith and Morgan in the catalogue of 1928–29), while Morgan was finally promoted to director of the School of Architecture. Labatut was a Frenchman, one of the most brilliant students in Laloux's atelier at the Ecole des Beaux-Arts, and a winner of the Second Grand Prix de Rome. With his arrival, the Princeton system really coalesced and became what it would remain until Morgan's resignation as director in 1954 and Labatut's retirement in 1967.

Thus, by 1928, when the damage of Butler's death had finally been overcome, a hybrid institution had emerged. On the one hand there was the link to the Department of Art and Archaeology, maintained as Butler had conceived it by Morgan and embodied in the young architectural historians who had grown up in the joint department and been added to the joint staff: Earl Baldwin Smith, Richard Stillwell, George Forsyth, and Donald Drew Egbert. On the other hand, there was a single design critic, Labatut, instead of Butler's system of ateliers, and that critic a Beaux-Arts man in addition.

Labatut, nonetheless, managed to fit in, and he did so by abstracting his Beaux-Arts philosophy to produce a more brilliant equivalent of Butler and Morgan's tergiversations on style. He had no significant practice until later in life, but if we look

---

51. Sherley Warner Morgan, Faculty Housing, Princeton University, Princeton, New Jersey, 1921. Facade. 52. Sherley Warner Morgan, Faculty Housing, Princeton University, Princeton, New Jersey, 1921. Facade detail.

52

51

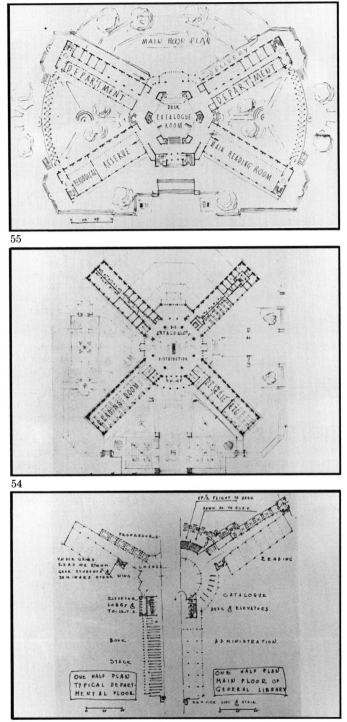

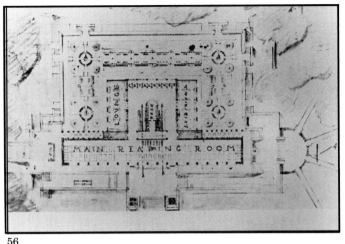

at some of the early projects executed under his tutelage, we find the greatest variety of solutions. In 1931—evidently by fortuitous chance—six of the M.F.A. theses all adopted the same program, "A Humanistic Library" (Figures 53–58). Four are in the monumental, stripped classical style of thirties classicism, one is in the light functional style of the Bauhaus, and one is Wrightian. They are the earliest indications of Labatut's principle of never dictating a style for a building, but instead, of talking about each problem until a solution can be chosen. That is, he presented architectural design as less a creative process than an evaluative one—one in which history (in many senses of that word) was the basis.

This eclecticism, however, extended beyond Labatut. It was a basic quality of the Princeton educational philosophy as it manifested itself in the Department of Art and Archaeology, especially in the work and teaching of the professors of architectural history: Smith, Stillwell, Forsyth, and especially Egbert. Since the latter's death in 1973 he has been looked upon as a peculiarly adventurous scholar, devoting most of his career to the study of the once-unpopular subjects of radical politics among artists and the teaching system of the Ecole des Beaux-Arts.[25] But, contrary to popular belief (and as is clear in the first pages of both of his volumes on these subjects) he was not an advocate of either Marxism or Beaux-Arts design. He merely presents these as significant points of view to be judged as one would any other. His ultimate objective—made very clear in his course lectures—was to lay out all the important points of view on art and design formulated during the period

53. Carter Hewitt, M.F.A. Thesis Project for a "Humanistic Library," Princeton University School of Architecture, 1931. Plan. 54. Charles K. Agle, M.F.A. Thesis Project for a "Humanistic Library," Princeton University School of Architecture, 1931. Plan. 55. William McMillan, M.F.A. Thesis Project for a "Humanistic Library," Princeton University School of Architecture, 1931. Plan. 56. George O'Bryan Bailey, M.F.A. Thesis Project for a "Humanistic Library," Princeton University School of Architecture, 1931. Plan. 57. R. A. Ruge, M.F.A. Thesis Project for a "Humanistic Library," Princeton University School of Architecture, 1931. Plan. 58. Vernon Kenneth Mangold, M.F.A. Thesis Project for a "Humanistic Library," Princeton University School of Architecture, 1931. Plan.

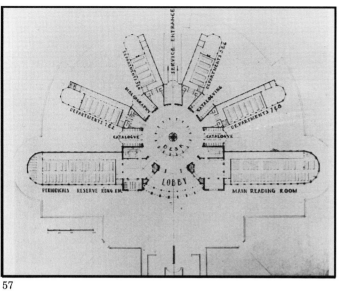

57

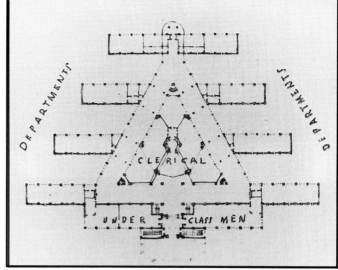

58

of his expertise, succinctly and accurately. His pedagogical detachment was imperturbable and, at the time of the crusade for Modernism, infuriating. Almost alone among American historians of modern architecture, he refused to take a polemical position and, in memory now, has not been left stranded by the erosion of the Modernist movement.

"I took Donald Drew Egbert's course on the History of Modern Architecture four times," writes Robert Venturi. "I sat in on it as a freshman, was the slide projectionist as a sophomore, took it for credit as a junior, and taught in it as a graduate student teaching assistant."[26] What he says he admired in Egbert's lectures was the evenness and clarity of his presentation of a vast range of material, undistorted by the need to make any polemical point. Venturi and the other architecture students thus were left space to select what they wished and to make their own points. And this would seem to have been the basic gift of the "Princeton system," if one unconsciously bestowed. With all its emphasis upon clarity and continuity, with all its resolute avoidance of taking a stand or overlooking something, it gave students an absolutely consistent basic body of knowledge which allowed the cleverest of them to adventure confidently on their own.

Notes

1. This essay, written by a 1965 graduate of the Department of Art and Archaeology and a draftsman on the Sardis Archaeological Expedition (1970–72), is as much a reminiscence as a piece of historical scholarship, and I am deeply indebted to several old friends for their memories and advice: Earl Coleman of the Princeton University Archives; Professors David Coffin and Robert Judson Clark of the department; Earl Baldwin Smith's son, Lacey Baldwin Smith, my senior colleague now at Northwestern University; Donald Drew Egbert's widow, Virginia Egbert Kilborne; and Howard Crosby Butler's descendants, Bettina Goosen and T. E. Blaiklock. I also owe thanks to Richard de Frances of North Salem, N.Y., for his help in tracing the Butler family.
I have also relied upon Marilyn Aronberg Lavin's history of the Department of Art and Archaeology, *The Eye of the Tiger* (Princeton: Princeton University Press, 1983), which expands the account of the department given by Allan Marquand in his dedicatory address of 1923, *Dedication of McCormick Hall* (Princeton: Princeton University Press, 1923).

2. Frank Jewett Mather elegantly profiles his life-long friend and colleague in the *Dictionary of American Biography,* vol. 12 (New York: Scribner's, 1943), pp. 291–92.

3. See the commemorative volume *Howard Crosby Butler, 1872–1922* (Princeton: Princeton University Press, 1923), and Henry F. Osborn, *Impressions of American Naturalists* (New York: Scribner's, 1925). I have also consulted the Butler materials preserved in the Princeton University archives, the Marquand Papers in Firestone Library, and other materials in the Expedition Room, Department of Art and Archaeology, the Harvard-Cornell Expedition to Sardis, and the hands of the family.

4. A contemporaneous exception that, in fact, proves the rule, was the University of Virginia, which in 1918 had placed Fiske Kimball in charge of its architecture program. He is known today as a historian and as the director of the Philadelphia Museum of Art. He was, however, a conventionally trained architect from Harvard. He had previously taught design at the University of Illinois and the University of Michigan. While at Virginia he designed a number of university buildings, most notably the gymnasium.

5. On McCormick Hall, see the dedication book cited in note 1, and Butler's article, "McCormick Hall and the School of Architecture," *Princeton Alumni Weekly,* November 2, 1921. Butler discusses the choice of style, saying that Cram offered three alternative projects in different styles, among which Italian Gothic was selected by the Trustees Committee on Grounds and Buildings and the Special Committee on the School of Architecture (of which latter committee Butler was the leading member) because
It would manifestly be unsuitable to erect in this particular corner of the campus a building in the [Collegiate Gothic] style of the Dining Halls. It would equally be out of place to choose a style from one of the buildings in the immediate neighborhood and push it forward in face of the opposition of the others. A medieval style was chosen by Mr. Cram, a style more neutral than Collegiate Gothic, friendly to Romanesque and Classic alike, and adaptable to almost any material or color scheme.

6. As is very evident from the letters they hurriedly exchanged, which are now preserved in the Marquand Papers at Firestone Library, Princeton University.

7. See David Littlejohn's biography of Moore, *Architect: The Life and Work of Charles W. Moore* (New York: Holt, Reinhart and Winston, 1984), pp. 117–27. Morgan's successor, Robert McLaughlin, however, was nonetheless himself a product of the School: B.A., 1923; M.F.A., 1926.

8. Butler anecdotes still circulate in great numbers at Princeton. A modest representative of the genre was written down by an early student of the graduate program and is reproduced in the 1923 memorial volume:
He was never hurried and never abrupt. He seemed to create an atmosphere of scholarly leisure; yet what a worker! He lectured twelve hours a week; he corrected personally and painstakingly a mass of notebooks; he superintended the whole running of the house [Merwick, where the Graduate School was located from 1905 to 1913]. Besides his formal duties he was drawing plates and ceaselessly

working on the publications springing from his archaeological researches. Not only was he publishing the results of past work but he was finding funds and making preparations of every sort for coming trips to the Near East. In addition to a scholarly mind, he possessed great organizing ability and a surprising power of doing two things at once. Often I have seen him taking part in a general conversation while the architectural plate grew in beauty and complexity beneath his calmly moving fingers.

9. The university catalogue for 1902–3 places his two courses under a separate heading, "Architecture," placed immediately after the Art and Archaeology offerings, and describes them thus:

ELEMENTS OF ARCHITECTURE   The Classic Orders, studied in their historic development, from reproductions of the ancient monuments, from the text of Vitruvius, from the works of Vignola; with drawings from restorations and photographs. . . .

CHRISTIAN ARCHITECTURE   A Practical Study of Ecclesiastical Architecture from the Fourth Century to the Twelfth, including the subjects of construction, design and details of the Early Christian, Byzantine and Romanesque periods

In 1903–4 a new course was added, "HISTORICAL DRAWING   The Classic Orders drawn to scale in pen and ink and in wash drawing, with shades and shadows. . . ." In 1904–5 these courses were integrated into the offerings of the Department of Art and Archaeology.

10. The catalogue description reads: "The application of classic architectural principles to the solution to problems in design suitable for beginners . . ." with "major design problems involving plans, elevations and sections. . . ."

11. He published Butler's *Early Churches in Syria* in 1929.

12. From a typescript by Butler submitted to Marquand for his approval and now preserved in the Marquand Papers, Firestone Library.

13. It should be noted that an atelier system had been established at Columbia in 1903, when A. F. D. Hamlin assumed the directorship, with one atelier at the university itself, conducted by Delano with Gumaer as his assistant, and two in offices in the city, conducted by Thomas Hastings (John Vreedenberg Van Pelt, assistant) and Charles McKim (John Russell Pope, assistant). T. K. Rohdenburg, *A History of the School of Architecture* (New York: Columbia University Press, 1954), Chapter 2.

14. Marquand Papers, Firestone Library, Princeton University.

15. Marquand Papers, Firestone Library, Princeton University.

16. Informal drawings of his exist in the possession of his family, while a number of his archaeological drawings survive in the Expedition Room in McCormick Hall. His illustrations to his Syrian volume are exquisite.

17. The *Princeton Alumni Weekly* of February 27, 1895, published the architect's rendering, by Debec and Chamberline of New York, together with news of its completion, and makes no mention of Butler's involvement. Butler's authorship is asserted by Varnum Lansing Collins in his necrology of him in the 1923 memorial volume.

18. The Presbyterian Church, which Richard de Frances tells me was the elaboration of an older wooden building moved to the site.

19. To these should be added the expedition building he erected at Sardis beginning in 1910, a rude if roomy affair attempting to respond to the local climatic conditions using local material and building techniques. He proudly publishes and explains it in the first of his Sardis volumes.

20. Paul Turner, *Campus: An American Planning Tradition* (Cambridge, Mass.: MIT Press, 1984), Chapter 6.

21. See, for example, his MS letter to the *Princeton Alumni Weekly*, preserved in his papers in the Princeton University Archives, on the subject of the style appropriate for the new university chapel. Here he attacks the suggestion that this should be a New England meeting house (because of its Calvinist implications for Presbyterian Princeton) and declares, "Princeton University has chosen for the style of its new buildings the type of architecture which represents the best artistic achievements of our Anglo-Saxon race and the only type ever devised solely for collegiate purposes."

22. Dean West and Butler were categorical about their monastic ideal, as is evident in several of their publications on the subject and in their MS critique of Cram's first, 1909 scheme for the building now in the Princeton University Archives.

23. My information comes from his file in the Princeton University Archives. Mather proposes his candidacy in a letter to Marquand of August 26, 1922, in the Marquand Papers, Firestone Library. His application for membership in the American Institute of Architects states that he was born in Enghien, France, in 1871, graduated in architecture from Columbia University in 1893, worked as a draftsman for Ernest Flagg for three years, for Carrere and Hastings for three years, and for Warren and Wetmore for one. The Princeton Archives documents state that he taught at Cornell from 1913 to 1915 and at Carnegie Institute from 1915 to 1923.

24. Again, I depend for my information upon his file in the Princeton University Archives. Joan Draper, who knows the Bennett papers in the Chicago Art Institute, informs me that there is at least one reference to d'Amato, in a letter of April 4, 1912. At that time Bennett was designing urban furniture for the first efforts to put the 1909 Chicago Plan, upon which project Bennett had been Burnham's principal assistant, into execution.

25. *Social Radicalism and the Arts* (New York: Knopf, 1970); *The Beaux-Arts Tradition in French Architecture* (Princeton: Princeton University Press, 1980).

26. In his "Tribute" introducing Egbert's posthumously published *Beaux-Arts Tradition*, xiii.

Robert Venturi and "The Return of Historicism"

Neil Levine, Harvard University

Among the many reasons why Robert Venturi can be considered the most influential architect alive today, perhaps first and foremost is his understanding of the role history must play in the restoration of a representational dimension to modern architecture. To discuss his work exclusively in terms of the appropriation of elements of pop culture and vernacular traditions seems to me to miss, or even purposely to conceal, that much more important point. Long before *Learning from Las Vegas* (1972), or even Levittown, came the first manifesto of what Nikolaus Pevsner was already bemoaning as "the return of historicism," Venturi's *Complexity and Contradiction in Architecture* (1966).[1] And even before that came Guild House, with its radical and prophetic use of the historical precedent of classical composition and detailing for what was, in effect, "merely" another example of economic modern housing.

Guild House, the apartment building in Philadelphia that was constructed between 1960 and 1963, was the first major design of Venturi's to be built and can appropriately be taken as the point of reference for this essay (Plate 1 and Figure 59). Its predominant segmental arch, ultimately deriving from Roman sources, became a leitmotif of his architecture as well as the basis for pastiche after pastiche by countless other designers over the next quarter century. The subsequent Vanna Venturi House (1961–64) (Plate 2 and Figure 10), Trubek House (1970–71) (Plate 3), and Wu Hall (1980–83) (Plate 7 and Figure 95) must all be seen in terms of the representational meaning Guild House gave to historical allusion as well as the specific contextual purpose that building first articulated for the revival of traditional forms and ideas of design.

The idea of historical precedent, which directed Venturi's very earliest projects, became the touchstone of his discussion of architectural theory in *Complexity and Contradiction in Architecture,* written after Guild House was designed and published three years after the building was completed. In his preface to the book, Venturi quoted T. S. Eliot to explain how tradition, meaning "the historical sense"—"a conscious sense of the past"—guided his own work,[2] and the hundreds of small photographs included in the margins of the text were meant to illustrate how, in Venturi's mind, an architect must draw on historical precedent in order to represent an architectural thought. That sense of historical precedent was shown to be as broad

and as eclectically based as one might imagine, with images on a single page (Figure 60), for instance, drawn from Gothic France, Baroque England, Mannerist Italy, Rococo Bavaria, Romantic-Classical London, ancient Rome, twentieth-century modernity as well as, and this is what is so important, twentieth-century historicism, the last represented by the photograph at the upper left of Brasini's Forestry Building at the E.U.R. site outside Rome. And, in the even later *Learning from Las Vegas,* Venturi's main theoretical contribution was an essay on architectural symbolism that differentiated traditional "representational art" from modern "abstract expressionism". according to the values of "Historical and Other Precedents" that might lead back "Towards an Old Architecture."[3] Here again, the expression and "symbolic meaning" to be associated with nineteenth-century stylistic revivals was put forth, still fairly radically for the time, as the all-important link in the chain of tradition that connected the twentieth century to the past.

Although Venturi may have been unique among architects in the wide range of his references to the past, as well as his positive valuation of the "eclecticism" over which the "purism" of the so-called Modern Movement had triumphed, he was hardly alone in the late 1950s and early 1960s in his desire to return architecture to some semblance of historical form. Indeed, at the very same time Guild House was going up, Venturi's former mentor Louis Kahn was completing the designs for the Meeting House and Living Quarters of the Salk Institute at La Jolla, which were to be faced with panels of Roman, travertine arches (Figure 78). Already by 1961, when Pevsner launched his attack on Neo-Historicism, describing it as "the belief in the power of history to such a degree as to choke original action and replace it by action which is inspired by period precedent,"[4] there was a plethora of examples of such buildings to point to, by Philip Johnson, Eero Saarinen, and Louis Kahn in the United States, or Franco Albini and Ignazio Gardella in Italy. The late work of both Wright and Le Corbusier was affected by such ideas (Figures 68–74), as were even some of the projects by Gropius's Architects' Collaborative. Everyone seemed to be aware of the need to reach beyond the Modernist dogma of pure functional expression.

The result, however, was by no means a single monolithic approach. Historical precedent could be revived for purely dec-

60

59. Venturi and Rauch, with Cope and Lippincott, Guild House, Philadelphia, Pennsylvania, 1960–63. Front facade. 60. Robert Venturi, Complexity and Contradiction in Architecture, *1966. Photographs on page 68.*

61

62

orative purposes, resulting in the ubiquitous, screen-like curtain walls of Yamasaki, Stone, and others. It could become a new, almost abstract Formalism, as numerous critics characterized Philip Johnson's designs of the time.[5] It could be used on a mostly ad hoc, purely contextual basis, as was so often the case in Italy. It could serve as a way of adjusting Modernist strategies to the desire for a "new monumentality."[6] By reading the present into the past, it could become a way of justifying a historicist basis for Modernist ahistoricism, just as it could also serve, by contrast, as the basis for a reinvestigation of the primitive roots of architectural forms and typologies.

From a theoretical point of view, two very distinct and divergent streams of thought developed, the one represented by the critic/architect Colin Rowe, and the other by the art historian Vincent Scully. Rowe's position, articulated in a number of pithy articles in the London-based *Architectural Review*, beginning in the late forties, was a revisionist view of history in which he maintained, contrary to popular belief, that history had in fact never been denied by the Modern Movement; it was just a bit "deconstructed." The Modernist architecture of the 1920s that had always prided itself on its freedom from the classical past was thus explained as a new form of classicism itself. In his "Mathematics of the Ideal Villa," published in 1947, Rowe argued with great effectiveness that Le Corbusier's private houses, such as the Villa Savoie or Villa Stein at Garches, followed the same essential principles of organization as Palladio's Villa Rotonda, and thus deserved to be considered as modern variants of the same classical ideal (Figures 61, 62).[7] Through this logic, the classical was disembodied of its traditional forms and associations. No direct historical references were any longer necessary since Modernism had arrived at the "thing in itself." And, even more to the point, since the very idea of classicism was abstracted from its historical context and forms, the notion of abstraction was given a kind of historical validity.

The purist logic in fact derived from Le Corbusier himself who, in his polemical writings of the twenties, had insisted on how the "regulating lines" of his proportioning system were essentially the same as those used in classical buildings of the past.[8] Photographs of Michelangelo's High Renaissance Campidoglio or Gabriel's mid-eighteenth-century Petit Trianon at

Versailles were reproduced in *Vers une architecture* with superimposed right triangles in order to clarify the analogy with his own designs (Figures 63, 64). But, that is not all these comparisons make evident, for Le Corbusier obviously meant to differentiate as much as to equate. In the case of Gabriel's garden pavilion, those black lines read not so much as overlapping triangles but as great Xs crossing out the columns and pediments and cornices of the classical building as if to suggest that they are not only frivolous and unnecessary, but also wrong— or, at least, would be so in the twentieth century. Indeed, the final message of *Vers une architecture* was that the only way to rival the past was to disencumber the present of its burden:

Architecture finds itself confronted with new laws. Construction has undergone innovations so great that the old "styles," which still obsess us, can no longer clothe it. . . . [T]he "styles" no longer exist, they are outside our ken; if they still trouble us, it is as parasites. If we set ourselves against the past, we are forced to the conclusion that the old architectural code, with its mass of rules and regulations evolved during four thousand years, is no longer of any interest; it no longer concerns us: all the values have been revised; there has been revolution in the conception of what Architecture is.[9]

The point on which Modernist theory and its revisionist version both agreed was the supposed bankruptcy of nineteenth-century eclecticism. Here is where the chain of history had been broken and the "styles" proved themselves to be a "lie,"[10] a stage set on which the eclectic architects of the nineteenth century played out their wildest fantasies and wish fulfillments in a dream turned nightmare (Figure 65). Alienated from the continuum of history by an interregnum of nearly two centuries, the very conception of history became in Rowe's

61. *Le Corbusier, Villa Stein, Garches, France, 1926–27.*
62. *Andrea Palladio, Villa Rotonda, Vicenza, Italy, begun circa 1567–69.   63. Le Corbusier, Villa Stein, Garches, France, 1926–27. Facade elevation with "regulating lines."   64. Le Corbusier, Photograph of A.-J. Gabriel's Petit Trianon at Versailles, France, with superimposed "regulating lines."   65. Thomas Cole,* The Architect's Dream, *oil on canvas, 1840.*

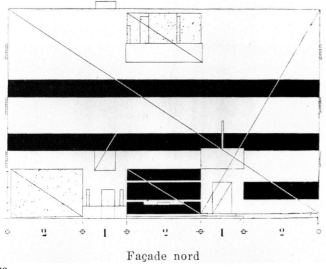

Façade nord

63

64

65

66   67

theory a complete abstraction. This strangely compelling historical amnesia of revisionist Modernism continued into the sixties and seventies ultimately to determine the battle lines drawn between what came to be called the "Whites"—the Modernist purists—and the "Greys"—those who evolved a more inclusive and more reasoned understanding of history and our connection to it through the lesson of Scully's thought and its intimate relation to the architecture of both Venturi and Kahn.[11]

In his book on *The Shingle Style,* written as a doctoral dissertation for Yale University in the late 1940s and published in 1955, Scully, like Rowe, addressed the problem of modern classicism. But instead of reading out most of the recent past, Scully tried to show the continuity of the classical tradition by bringing it up to date, across the nineteenth century and well into the twentieth, with the work of McKim, Mead and White and Frank Lloyd Wright.[12] He pictured history not as an alien world to which one only has access through a highly intellectualized process of analogy and abstraction, but rather as a world that has informed our own, through the local character and vernacular quality of the architecture in which we grew up. Scully himself showed how Venturi's architecture early on expressed this direct and organic connection to history, most particularly in the house he designed for his mother in 1961 (Figure 10).[13] This, Scully related to Frank Lloyd Wright's own house in Oak Park of 1889 (Figure 13), and then on back to Bruce Price's Shingle Style cottages in Tuxedo Park of a few years before (Figure 12). In all of them, the representational elements of the classical tradition were shown to have been used in such a way as to condense the image of shelter into a traditionally recognizable form. Stylistic references to Palladio or Serlio were not direct but filtered through more than three centuries of continuous experience, and thus continually transformed by the changing local conditions and materials.

Throughout his scholarly and critical writings of the fifties and sixties, ranging over subjects as diverse as Greek architecture, Michelangelo, Louis Kahn, and Frank Lloyd Wright, Scully presented the relation between the modern experience and the historical past as sympathetic rather than adversarial. Kahn, he liked to point out, was "trained in the Beaux-Arts to regard the buildings of the past as friends rather than as ene-

mies."[14] This attitude toward the past, which Venturi clearly shared with Scully and Kahn, was no longer simply traditionalism. By then, it took a wholly new, less dogmatic view of modern architecture to see how to reintegrate the present with the past. During the high moment of Modernism in the first half of this century, most of the forms and organizational patterns of traditional architecture had in fact been jettisoned in the hope of arriving at something unforeseen, a new architecture that would be specifically appropriate to the machine age. Wright called his Larkin Building of 1903–6 (Figure 66) the "Great Protestant" and described its interlocking, nearly abstract cubic forms as "negating" all historical reference.[15] In Le Corbusier's Villa Savoie (Figure 67), that abstract idea of pure forms in space was taken to a logical conclusion, and the modern notion of an architecture totally responsive to its own internal factors of material, program, and space was given its "classic" (not classical) statement. The open plan, free-flowing space, clear rectilinear form, and reinforced concrete structure all offered an image of architecture totally unhooked from the past and, indeed, from everything around it. This *was* the ideal of Modernism, "the thing in itself."

Naturally, as the free plan, the free facade, the idea of *pilotis,* and what Colin Rowe liked to call "peripheric composition"[16] came to be synonymous with modernity, the single most regressive form that might be revived from a premodern condition was the arch, or its extension as a dome or vault. Of all those elements banished from the canon of modern design, the arch was one of the first that had to go. It spoke of the weight of tradition, of massive structural systems of masonry, of hierarchy and symmetry, of closure and formal classical order. It also spoke of connectedness to everything around it, and to everything that preceded it in time and space. Where Scully would see in the arches of Kahn or Venturi a "gesture" full of

---

66. Frank Lloyd Wright, Larkin Building, Buffalo, New York, 1903–6. Foundation; in Architectural Record, *March 1908.) 67. Le Corbusier, Villa Savoie, Poissy, France, 1928–30. 68. Le Corbusier, Roq and Rob Housing Development project, Cap Martin, France, 1949. Sketch. 69. Frank Lloyd Wright, Lloyd Burlingham House project, El Paso, Texas, 1942. Plot plan with perspective and elevation sketches.*

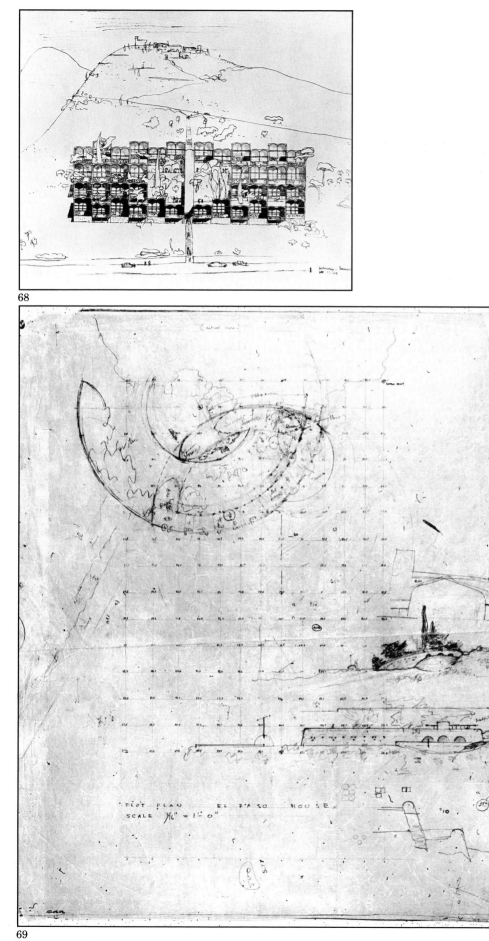

68

69

70

rich human possibilities, Rowe described such "episodic blisters" as "sclerotic" and "regressive" in terms of the machine aesthetic.[17]

As a gauge of the general movement back to historical precedent in the post-war period, it is significant then that both Le Corbusier and Wright began to use arches and vaults in various projects, although in very different ways—Wright tending to emphasize more and more the representational character of the motif and Le Corbusier tending to stress its purely structural possibilities at the expense of any historical associations. In the 1940s, Le Corbusier designed a number of buildings, such as the Roq and Rob housing community (Figure 68) on the Mediterranean coast of France, using a system of segmental, Catalan vaults, inspired by local traditions of masonry construction, and building on some of his experiments of the previous two decades. By contrast, Wright used the arch in a much more explicitly historicizing way, to express the connection with local history, in a project for a house in El Paso, Texas, of 1942, that was to have been built in adobe (Figure 69).

This difference between the structural expression of Le Corbusier's return to the arch and Wright's more representational use became clearer in the later forties and fifties. In his Maisons Jaoul (Figure 70), built in the wealthy Neuilly suburb of Paris in the mid-fifties, Le Corbusier stressed the archaizing, primitive nature of the sheltering vault and, as in the Roq and Rob project, merely indicated the arch on the exterior as an extrusion of the vault. It is almost as if, though drawn to the arch, Le Corbusier had to rationalize its use in a contemporary situation by denying its imagistic content. In the vaulted structures of his most important and monumental buildings of the period, such as the High Court at Chandigarh, or the Chapel of Notre-Dame-du-Haut at Ronchamp, both of the early 1950s, Le Corbusier went so far as to subvert the traditional meaning of the arched shape. At Chandigarh (Figure 71), the continuous vault of the roof is strictly contained within a rectilinear framework that defines the expressive charge of the building, thus

70. Le Corbusier, Maisons Jaoul, Neuilly-sur-Seine, France, 1954–56.   71. Le Corbusier, High Court of Justice, Chandigarh, India, 1951–56.   72. Le Corbusier, Chapel of Notre-Dame-du-Haut, Ronchamp, France, 1950–55. Interior.

71

72

73

74

75

76

relegating the vault to a purely structural condition. In the chapel at Ronchamp (Figure 72), the normally soaring vault of a church is turned upside down to create a sense of implosion and cause the space to be felt not as something contained but rather as something pushing down and out.

In his 1948 design for the Morris Store (Figure 73), in San Francisco, Wright, on the other hand, accepted the traditional function of the arch as an expression of entrance and used its continuous form to urbanistic purpose, helping to link his building to the others along the narrow, downtown street. In the Marin County Civic Center (Figure 74) of ten years later, his last major building, Wright went even further in treating the arched shape as a purely symbolic cutout, with no structural reason other than that of representation. Making direct reference to a Republican Roman aqueduct such as the Pont du Gard, near Nîmes, Wright accepted the precedent of historical form as a means of conveying the image of civic purpose in public works.

Following the example of such "form-givers" as Le Corbusier and Wright, as well as the cryptoclassical designs of engineers like Nervi, Maillart, and Candela, architects throughout the world in the 1950s picked up on this use of the arch for both structural and representational purposes. For Saarinen in his Chapel at MIT (Figure 75), it helped create the image of a stripped-down, late antique baptistry, stranded in a land of technology; for Oscar Niemeyer in his Presidential Palace at Brasilia (Figure 76), it gave a certain expression of pomp to an otherwise emaciated Chandigarh. The abstracted, inverted arcade is used as a screen and could thus be rationalized, in functional terms, as a decorative *brise-soleil,* or sun-break, in Corbusian terminology.

Of all the architects who experimented with the arch in the 1950s, Louis Kahn undoubtedly came closest to providing a serious rationale for its reincorporation in modern architecture

as an element of structural clarity as well as a form of rich, symbolic significance. Between 1959 and 1961, Kahn designed both the U.S. Consulate in Luanda, Angola, and the Meeting House and Staff Living Quarters for the Salk Institute for Biological Studies in La Jolla, in which he used the flat, cutout shape of the arch in a new and powerful way (Figures 77, 78). In both projects, the large-scale Roman arch with its light slot below creates, in a structurally integral way, the facade of the building while at the same time detaching itself from the structure to function as a light-diffusing screen, again a Corbusian *brise-soleil* in effect. In Luanda, the flat, arched screens are set up along the flanks of the consulate under the overhanging roof "umbrella," protecting the interior from the glare of the sun just as the roof would keep out the rain.

The form of an arch piercing the plane of the wall to provide a soft, mysterious sense of light had other poetic connotations for Kahn, however, which depended on certain historical associations with Roman vaulted construction that were inspired by the melancholic nature of ruins. Kahn described these designs of his as resulting from the idea of "wrapping ruins around buildings."[18] In the Salk Meeting House, in particular, one can read Kahn's design as a kind of recycling of the past in which rooms of circular and square plan have been reconstructed and inserted within an existing Roman fabric of curving and straight arched planes. At this poetic level of interpretation, then, the notion of using the ruin as a model for retrieving history allows the modern architect rationally to reinvest his work with the past without having to accept all of it fully. The ruin represents only part of what once existed: it exhibits what remains of the past once time and the forces of nature have done their work to reduce the complete body of the building to a mere skeleton (Figure 79).

Kahn's historicism still reveals a profound allegiance to Modernist thought in its prohibition against decoration or ornament, that is to say, in its proscription of what can be thought of as extraneous to the structural order of the building. One can therefore read Kahn's notion of the ruin as a poetic justification for the idea of getting back to basics, an idea which was at the heart of the modern theory of structural rationalism so eloquently propounded in the later nineteenth century by Viollet-le-Duc. As Viollet explained in his comparative analysis of Greek,

73. Frank Lloyd Wright, Morris Store, San Francisco, California, 1948–49. 74. Frank Lloyd Wright, Marin County Civic Center, San Rafael, California, 1957–70. 75. Eero Saarinen, Chapel, Massachusetts Institute of Technology, Cambridge, Massachusetts, 1951–55. 76. Oscar Niemeyer, Presidential Palace (Palace of the Dawn), Brasilia, Brazil, 1956–59.

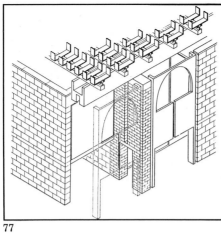

77

78

Roman, and Gothic architecture, the trabeated, decorative treatment of Roman buildings was entirely extraneous to the underlying structural order of arches and vaults.[19] In order to assess such works at their true value, the architect had to try to imagine these great engineering marvels stripped of all ornament. Drawings such as the *Analysis of Roman Baths* he produced for the history course at the Ecole Spéciale d'Architecture in the 1860s illustrate the stages in the actual process of construction (Figure 80). Reading from left to right, we can see how the underlying brick skeleton of arches and vaults was "masked" by the added layer of historic decoration. Viollet's modern, X-ray vision, however, allows us to "see through" the mistakes of history, for with hindsight we can also read the drawing backwards, from right to left, deconstructing the building so to speak, in order to arrive at a more elemental and truthful level of information. The underlying brick and concrete structure of the building is what makes the building "what it wants to be," in Louis Kahn's terms, whereas the overlay of columns and entablatures is merely a rhetorical gesture, an unnecessary and, in the end, dissimulating device denying an expression of internal truth and authenticity.

When, in the 1960s, beginning with his work at Dacca, Kahn was able to put this historical theory of design into practice, the result was an architecture of elemental power and integrity. In the library at Phillips Exeter Academy (Figure 81), Kahn once again made load-bearing brick walls of Roman arched construction serve as an outer casing for the enormous concrete void at the center. Here, in effect, was a historical precedent of the most "regressive" sort used to fulfill the archetypally modern idea of the building standing alone as an object, a thing in itself, internally consistent, and entirely self-contained. History, in the process, was somehow denuded, for something was obviously left out. Buildings like the Exeter Library almost immediately looked, if not literally like ruins, then like something existing in a state of arrested development, in a process of becoming that is not yet complete. Kahn's library is like looking at the Viollet drawing of a Roman bath with a blinder over your right eye. There is a reference to the past, but to a past that will never be allowed to come into its own. Exeter Library has four faces but no facade; a central hall without a dedicated purpose; an enclosed portico with nothing to connect to.

It is against the idealism and hermeticism of Kahn's fully mature work[20] that Venturi's significance can best be appreciated, for it seems to me that one of the most important things Venturi did was to take off the blinders and look at the full historical picture, from the left all the way to the right. Thus he began to put back into that picture the signifying elements of representation that allow architecture to function as part of a larger social and urban form of discourse. In the house he built for his mother in 1961–64, just outside Philadelphia, the decorative features are explicitly applied to read as if appliquéd (Figure 82). Unlike the Exeter Library, where the integral and self-contained nature of the structural order is all-important, in the Vanna Venturi House, the parts of the building, as they relate to external factors, pull away from the whole, denying its internal consistency and thus distinguishing themselves in purely representational terms. In this process of returning to the idea of making a *facade* that would be a singular thing, different from any other part of the building and thus necessarily marked by certain features normally associated with the passage from the public realm into a more private one, Venturi soon came to the realization that he was transgressing a fundamental principle of Modernism. Instead of considering the building in isolation and designing it uniquely from the inside out, Venturi had reversed the process to take both sides into account. "Designing from the outside in," he later explained in *Complexity and Contradiction in Architecture,*

as well as the inside out, creates the necessary tensions, which help make architecture. Since the inside is different from the outside, the wall—the point of change—becomes an architectural event. Architecture occurs at the meeting of interior and exterior forces of use and space. These interior and environmental forces

77. Louis I. Kahn, U.S. Consulate project, Luanda, Angola, 1959. Chancellery, isometric of side wall.   78. Louis I. Kahn, Meeting House project, Salk Institute for Biological Studies, La Jolla, California, begun 1959. Perspective.   79. Giovanni Battista Piranesi, Baths of Caracalla, *etching.   80. Eugène-Emmanuel Viollet-le-Duc,* Analysis of Roman Baths, *lithograph, mid-1860s.   81. Louis I. Kahn, Library, Phillips Exeter Academy, Exeter, New Hampshire, 1965–72.*

79

81

83

are both general and particular, generic and circumstantial. Architecture as the wall between the inside and the outside becomes the partial record of this resolution and its drama.[21]

"And by recognizing the difference between the inside and the outside," Venturi concluded, "architecture opens the door once again to an urbanistic point of view."[22]

The Vanna Venturi House presents to the path that leads in from the street a traditional facade in order to create a sense of continuity with the suburban environment. The gable and arch over the central entrance are indications of shelter and invitations readily understood from a distance. The difference between Venturi's conception of how a house should relate to its context and Kahn's view of the same problem is quite striking when we compare the Vanna Venturi House to the abstract, almost completely inward-looking design of Kahn's nearly contemporary Fisher House of 1960 (Figure 83), located in the nearby suburb of Hatboro, or his Esherick House of 1959–61, located just down the street from Venturi's mother's house. But it is perhaps only in the even earlier Guild House, designed for a truly urban situation, that one can begin to see not only how far Venturi diverged from Kahn but also how much the factor of historical representation had to do with his search for a more contextual architecture.

Guild House is located on a main thoroughfare of Philadelphia, not quite a boulevard but still a significant street. The rear of the brick-clad structure is almost completely undistinguished and looks like a fairly straightforward piece of pragmatic, functional design (Figure 84). As it turns the corner, however, a very slight, though evident change occurs at the next-to-top-floor level of windows (Figure 85). The more the building opens up to the street, however, the more the white line of bricks, which is at first a bit difficult to understand, becomes clearly legible as a historical sign indicating a stringcourse. It is just a trace, but still something extra, added on. The apartment house then narrows in from its broad rear through a series of breaks and chamfers that finally telescope the build-

82. Venturi and Rauch, Vanna Venturi House, Chestnut Hill, Philadelphia, Pennsylvania, 1961–64. Front and side facades.
83. Louis I. Kahn, Fisher House, Hatboro, Pennsylvania, 1960.

84

85

86

ing into a central pavilion that meets the line of the street (Figure 86). Here, the white stringcourse near the cornice stops; but at the street level, where the building meets the ground, a nearly two-story plane of white brick brings the historical imagery down to ground level onto the support of a freestanding, axially placed, black column (Plate 1).

The entrance pavilion, with its overriding arched shape, magnifies the historical reference and brings the entire building into focus at the plane of the street. In contrast to Kahn's Exeter Library, where the generalized reference to Roman construction is diffused in equal parts throughout the building, and therefore diluted nearly beyond recognition, the specific historical references in Guild House are concentrated at the point where the building comes into direct contact with the street. The rhythm and progression from abstract functional form to explicit historical allusion are so subtle, yet so marked, that one cannot help but realize that Venturi was making a very simple yet profound point in this, his first major building.

The arch and the arcade have traditionally been associated in urban terms with the idea of making a street. As Venturi surely learned during the time he spent in Italy, an arcade might be used to connect disparate buildings along the street while, at the same time, through the device of a triumphal motif, an axis of approach to a major public monument might be marked with suitable fanfare (Figure 87). Although it is obvious in his design of Guild House that Venturi understood the significance of the arch as an element that can both define a street-line and indicate a point of entry into a more private space, more important than the specific determination of elements is the very fact that it was only at the street-line, the point where the building comes into direct contact with the

87

84. Venturi and Rauch, with Cope and Lippincott, Guild House, Philadelphia, Pennsylvania, 1960–63. Rear facade. 85. Venturi and Rauch, with Cope and Lippincott, Guild House, Philadelphia, Pennsylvania, 1960–63. Corner view of rear and side facades. 86. Venturi and Rauch, with Cope and Lippincott, Guild House, Philadelphia, Pennsylvania, 1960–63. Front facade along Spring Garden Street. 87. Piazza Malphigi, Bologna, Italy. View of square, with apse of S. Francesco on the right.

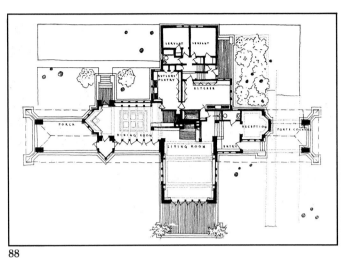

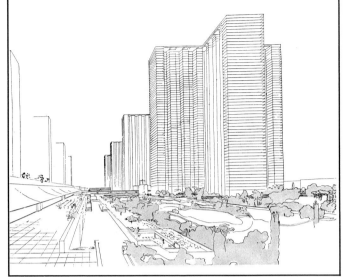

88   89

public frame of reference, that Venturi concentrated the historical devices he used. It was as if he was saying that, when a building takes its place in the public realm, it must begin to use a language of conventional reference and meaning in order to articulate its relation to the preexisting conditions; and, in doing that, it necessarily becomes part of history.

Indeed, one can see the stripping away of historical reference from the body of modern architecture as concomitant with the withdrawal of modern buildings from any determinative connection with the surrounding environment. The evolution of Wright's planning, for instance, from his houses of the 1890s to the mature Prairie Style, as illustrated in his Ward Willits House of 1901–2 (Figure 88), shows how he arrived at a modern, integral sense of interpenetrating space by centering his design on the intersection of axes out of which the peripheric composition develops. The pinwheel action around the central fireplace determines the flow of space, which can be read as expanding infinitely outward. In Le Corbusier's seminal city planning projects of the 1920s (Figure 89), the cruciform shapes of the prismatic glass towers likewise symbolize the growth of an architectural idea out of its own internal factors of program and construction, without any need to refer to external factors such as context or history. His iconic image of the Dom-ino system of reinforced concrete construction (Figure 90), drawn in 1914, makes the elemental purity of this idea absolutely transparent. A totally rational structural grid, answering to its own laws, is set up, in isolation, as the basis for a completely indeterminate system of free planning, eventually to be encased by a free facade. The world is treated as a *tabula rasa* upon which the architect can start from scratch. Structure, program, and materials become the purely internal factors that govern design.

The ultimate outcome of this Modernist idea, that each spe-

88. Frank Lloyd Wright, Ward Willits House, Highland Park, Illinois, 1901–2. Plan.   89. Le Corbusier, Contemporary City for 3 Million People project, 1922–25. Perspective.   90. Le Corbusier, Model of the Dom-ino System, 1914.   91. Kevin Roche, John Dinkeloo and Associates, Richard C. Lee High School, New Haven, Connecticut, 1962–67.   92. Moshe Safdie, Habitat, Montreal, Quebec, Canada, 1967.

92

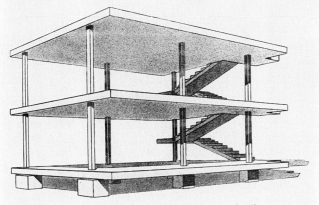

L'ossature standard « Dom-ino », pour exécution en grande série

90

91

94

cialized medium should acknowledge only those factors that are peculiar to itself and not shared by any other, reached a high point of development in the Brutalist architecture of the late 1950s and early 1960s. The *withdrawal* of Kevin Roche's Richard C. Lee High School in New Haven (Figure 91), or Moshe Safdie's Habitat for the Montreal Expo (Figure 92), for instance, could be rationalized as the result of a totally logical system of planning, programming, or construction technique, but the result of such thinking was catatonic, and catastrophic for the urban environment. In trying to heal these wounds, it soon became clear that piazzas would not help, for they almost immediately become moats, further separating the building from its urban context (Figures 93, 94). The fact may just well be that, despite all the talk of *pilotis* and *brise-soleils* as constituting a new formal vocabulary to replace that of the past, modern architecture never was able to develop a coherent language for articulating the relation between the building and its site as a form of public discourse. Isolated, autonomous, and self-centered, modern architecture seemed to offer no system of detailing, of relating part to part, that might serve as a way of informing and connecting that which is new with that which already exists. This, I think, is what Venturi understood before everyone else—and this is the ultimate lesson of Guild House.

In Guild House (Plate 1), as is perhaps even more true of the house he did for his mother, Venturi historicized Kahn's philosophy of "form" and "design."[23] Kahn's abstract geometric order was given an explicit historical image, while the circumstantial impact of function was shaped to meet the contingencies of location and use.[24] In this interaction of forces coming from without and within, the idea of the facade reemerged in architecture with all its traditional significance of distinction and pronouncement. This willingness on the part of Venturi to let the building share some part of its meaning with the context around it, and preceding it, owed its origins to his belief in the continuity of history as a tradition which, in T. S. Eliot's sense, never could be broken for it was always being remade. In accepting nineteenth-century architecture, and not just its engineering, as part of the modern condition, Venturi was able

to begin thinking about reinvesting form with the values of what he would call "explicit 'denotative' symbolism."[25]

In Guild House, as even more in Venturi's later buildings such as Wu Hall at Princeton (Plate 7 and Figure 95), we are presented with an architecture that perhaps more than any other of our time attempts to accommodate itself to preexisting conditions. For that reason, it seems, it has come to rely more and more on explicit historical details and references. And so Venturi's architecture ultimately raises a fundamental question of our times: Is it not inevitable that modern architecture must return to the use of historical form in order to relate to what is around it? In Wu Hall, the keystones, the heraldic pattern over the entrance, the gentle Tudor-Gothic bay windows, as well as the stone balls at the base of the steps all seem naturally to define a set of paths through the Princeton campus that no previous modern building was able to do (Figure 96). How much do the historical references have to do with this? Perhaps more than we think. But then, how literal do such allusions have to be?

Whereas Venturi was quite alone in 1960 in his understanding of historicism as a means toward representation, that is obviously not the case today. The range of references now extends from the most intensely literal and reconstructive classicism of an Allan Greenberg or a Leon Krier through the more contextually based choices of a James Stirling to the large-scale, prefabricated images of a Bofill to the simplified abstractions of an Aldo Rossi. All, however, are involved in one way or another with using the past to make an architecture of accommodation and association. While it is clearly too sweeping a statement to say that Venturi alone was responsible for this present state of affairs, I think it can safely be said that it was his early work, such as the Guild House, that made us aware that the "return of historicism" was as far from a loss of originality as it was from a strategy for justifying the inadequacies of the most recent past. Nor could it remain at the level of an abstraction; for as a means to representation, its ultimate purpose was in the realm of public discourse, signaling a revitalization of cultural memory and a desire for urban reform. And whatever ironies were once felt necessary by Venturi to maintain that position in a situation of "alarming" loss of faith in the present, as Pevsner felt the case to be in 1961,[26] are surely

---

93. Hugh Stubbins and Associates, Citicorp Center, New York, New York, 1977. 94. Street Scene in Downtown Dallas, Texas.

95

96

no more the case a quarter of a century later. The unself-conscious directness with which Venturi has dedicated his architecture, most recently at Princeton and now in London, to a supple and easy-going continuity with the past makes it abundantly clear how beliefs have changed, so that perhaps even the quotation marks may already be unnecessary when referring to history.

Notes

1. See Nikolaus Pevsner, "The Return of Historicism," originally published in the *Journal of the Royal Institute of British Architects*, 3rd ser., vol. 68, 1961; reprinted in N. Pevsner, *Studies in Art, Architecture and Design*, vol. 2: *Victorian and After* (London: Thames and Hudson, 1968), pp. 242–59.

2. Robert Venturi, *Complexity and Contradiction in Architecture*, with an introduction by Vincent Scully, Museum of Modern Art Papers on Architecture, no. 1 (New York: Museum of Modern Art, in association with the Graham Foundation for Advanced Studies in the Fine Arts, 1966), pp. 18–19.

3. Robert Venturi, Denise Scott Brown, and Steven Izenour, *Learning from Las Vegas* (Cambridge, Mass.: MIT Press, 1972), pp. 72–73.

4. Pevsner, *Studies in Art, Architecture and Design*, p. 243.

5. Cf. Jürgen Joedicke, *Architecture Since 1945: Sources and Directions* (New York: Frederick A. Praeger Publishers, 1969), pp. 139 ff.

6. The phrase, *a new monumentality*, was first used in this sense by Sigfried Giedion in "The Need for a New Monumentality," in *New Architecture and City Planning*, ed. Paul Zucker (New York: Philosophical Library, 1944), pp. 549–68.

7. Reprinted in Colin Rowe, *The Mathematics of the Ideal Villa and Other Essays* (Cambridge, Mass.: MIT Press, 1976), pp. 1–27.

8. Le Corbusier, *Towards a New Architecture*, trans. Frederick Etchells (orig. pub. 1923; ppb. ed., New York: Holt, Rinehart, and Winston, n.d.), pp. 63–79.

9. *Ibid.*, pp. 266–68.

10. *Ibid.*, p. 27.

11. See Robert A. M. Stern, "Stomping at the Savoye," *Architectural Forum* 138 (May 1973): 46–48.

12. Vincent J. Scully, Jr., *The Shingle Style: Architectural Theory and Design from Richardson to the Origins of Wright* (New Haven, Conn.: Yale University Press, 1955), pp. 113 ff.

13. See, e.g., his introduction to Venturi, *Complexity and Contradiction*, p. 13; and his *The Shingle Style Today, or the Historian's Revenge* (New York: George Braziller, 1974), esp. pp. 26–32.

14. V. Scully, *Louis I. Kahn* (New York: George Braziller, 1962), p. 11.

15. Frank Lloyd Wright, *An Autobiography*, rev. and enl. ed. (New York: Horizon Press, 1977), pp. 174–76.

16. Rowe, *Mathematics of the Ideal Villa*, pp. 128 ff. ("Neo-'Classicism' and Modern Architecture I," orig. pub. 1973).

17. *Ibid.*, pp. 150, 154, 156 ("Neo-'Classicism' and Modern Architecture II," orig. pub. 1973).

18. "Kahn," an interview in *Perspecta* 7 (1961): 9.

19. See, e.g., Eugène-Emmanuel Viollet-le-Duc, *Discourses on Architecture*, vol. 1, orig. pub. 1863; trans. Henry Van Brunt (Boston: James R. Osgood and Company, 1975).

20. Such an interpretation of Kahn's later work, like so much else in this essay, derives from Vincent Scully's lectures, and writings of the period, as well as numerous discussions with him on the subject of Kahn and Venturi.

21. Venturi, *Complexity and Contradiction*, pp. 88–89.

22. *Ibid.*, p. 89.

23. For the clearest statement of Kahn's philosophy, see his "Form and Design," originally recorded for the Voice of America *Forum Lectures*, 1960; reprinted in Scully, *Kahn*, pp. 114–21.

24. For Venturi's translation of Kahn's design method, see his discussion of the house for his mother in *Complexity and Contradiction*, pp. 117–21.

25. Venturi, *Learning from Las Vegas*, p. 72.

26. Pevsner, *Studies in Art, Architecture and Design*, p. 243.

95. Venturi, Rauch and Scott Brown, Gordon Wu Hall, Princeton University, Princeton, New Jersey, 1980–83. General view from the south. 96. Venturi, Rauch and Scott Brown, Gordon Wu Hall, Princeton University, Princeton, New Jersey, 1980–83. Front facade along entrance path.

Association and Dissociation: The Trubek and Wislocki Houses

Thomas Beeby, Yale University

"Nantucket . . . look at it," says Ishmael in *Moby Dick,* "—a mere hillock, and elbow of sand; all beach, without a background." The ocean that carried the whaler around the world in search of his prey pounds on the precious sands of this fabled island. The shoreline of New England became a favorite subject for the Luminist painters, for here the sublime expanse of sea, sand, and grass revealed the nature of the American God. These shores were the haven sought by the elect of New England in which to found an empire based on Puritan values. New England was the promised Eden at the end of the long journey of tribulation that separated the colonists from the sin of the Old World. Man-made objects placed in this vast landscape display at once qualities of heroic isolation and poignant temporality.

A myth of origins is basic to all men. It is a constant grounded in concerns of a most profound spiritual need. Its presence is felt in the highest artistic speculation as well as in the most mundane daily activity. A great deal of attention has been given to the image of the primitive wooden hut as the apology for classicism that Laugier used in his *Essai sur l'architecture* (1755) (Figure 97). Systematic reconstructions based on archaeological study provide other images that capture the imagination of architects. The shelters of Native American cultures offer other examples of iconic simplicity.

To the American mind, particularly for those not educated in the intricacies of stylistic developments, there is a continuing fixation on the Colonial houses of New England (Figure 98) as the heart of American sensibilities and values. Nantucket alone (Figure 99) has over eight hundred houses, built between 1740 and 1840, which developed through economic change a vernacular style that was almost completely free from the mid-nineteenth-century revivals. The Shingle Style (Figure 103) reinforced this earlier tradition by maintaining the forms and associations of Colonial architecture. The elements that make up this architectural tradition, as well as its related furnishings, maintain a magic hold on the American imagination.

The Trubek and Wislocki Houses of 1970–71 by Robert Venturi on Nantucket Island (Plate 3) engage the symbols and language of this legacy in a revolutionary and instructive manner that suggests a possibility for an American architecture that could be as powerful and central to this country as Herman Melville's *Moby Dick* (1851) has proven to be. The dialogue set up between the two tiny dwellings resonates between past and future, poetically illuminating the present.

When viewed from the land, the houses seem at first to be more similar than they actually are. The luminous sky, obliterating the fenestration and confusing detail, reduces the houses to two peaked blocks on the shoreline. The silhouette of each has a deep resonance, for they are volumetrically the progeny of the first houses of New England.

The smaller Wislocki House is taller and thinner than its companion; its overall configuration approaches the profile of the two-story hall and parlor houses that were one room deep (Figure 100). These houses have an awkward, ungainly presence that is stabilized by the chimney mass that ties the house to the land. No details project from the simple volume. The Wislocki House stands in proud defiance against the elements, unprotected and vulnerable, but the masonry core that gives the structure stability is missing. The symbolic heart of the house has been cut out. In its place, a fragile sheet-metal cylinder capped by louvers projects through the slope of the roof—abandoning the central position once occupied by the chimney on the ridge angle.

The second and larger house, the Trubek House, when seen from the access approach, is now understood to be wider and shallower than its companion. It is skewed slightly in relation to the Wislocki House to increase the intensity of their dialogue as distinct objects. The house assumes a volume closely resembling the later houses of New England that were two stories high and two rooms deep (Figure 101). Gone is the precarious height associated with the hall and parlor houses. In its place is a more ample sense of the structure resting on the ground. Yet missing again is the masonry block that once organized the house as it sprang from the earth to rise into the sky.

There is also a sense, established by the width of the end facade, that this house has an ancestor in the one-story Cape Cod houses (Figure 102) that hug the sand and maintain a firm grip on the shoreline. The iconic power of the Cape Cod cottage

---

97. *Marc-Antoine Laugier,* Essai sur l'architecture, *1755. Frontispiece. 98. Fairbanks House, Dedham, Massachusetts, 1637. 99. Nantucket, Nantucket Island, Massachusetts.*

97

99

98

101

102

100

103

has long had a sentimental position in the American dream. The loss of the central chimney at the Trubek House is therefore particularly painful, for without its central focus much of the power of the image has been drained. The Trubek House also suggests a relationship in profile to the later Shingle Style houses of the New England shoreline (Figure 103). Drawing on Colonial architecture for its vocabulary of forms and materials, the Shingle Style freely interpreted Colonial architecture to create a revolutionary style of true originality even while it maintained many of the sentimental attachments related to the mood and character of the earlier houses. The dominant features of this style, such as the shingle surfaces, edge details, and gable ends, are all consistent with both the Trubek House and the eighteenth-century houses found on Nantucket. Seen against the sky, the apparently simple volumes of the Trubek and Wislocki Houses suggest the familiar and reassuring ambience found in America's most beloved houses on Nantucket Island, Martha's Vineyard, and Cape Cod.

The Colonial Revival inaugurated by the Shingle Style has remained a powerful force in American residential design. The mood and imagery found in the photographs of Wallace Nutting from the beginning of this century are subtle propaganda for the dominance of Colonial architecture in the American home; the photographs firmly attempt to reestablish New England as this country's mythical place of origin. Twentieth-century residences by such architects as Royal Barry Wills were widely published and sustained public interest in the Colonial Revival against the attacks of Modernism. Yet the majority of houses built since the 1930s in this country are pale versions of their antecedents (Figure 104). Drained of any creative energy, preserving only minimal emaciated detailing in the face of economic constraints, they betray a steady decline in the artistic value of the Colonial Revival Style.

The Trubek and Wislocki Houses (Figures 105–7) also show the effects of economic constraints. A closer examination re-

100. Parson Capen House, Topsfield, Massachusetts, 1683. 101. Two-story house, South Yarmouth, Cape Cod, Massachusetts, n.d. 102. Standish House, Halifax, Massachusetts, 1730. 103. Shingle Style house, New London, Connecticut, late nineteenth century.

veals, however, that they are not suffering from the pursuit of an exhausted tradition. The two entry facades contradict the impressions created by the silhouettes and volumes of the houses. The Wislocki House has what is clearly an entrance on its south, gable-end facade (Figure 107). The central position of this door, surrounded by symmetrical fenestration and approached by an oversized stair, suggests that this could be the primary entry to the house. The front door of the Trubek House is less clear, for while the only visible door also appears on the south, gable end, its treatment suggests that it is only a service entrance (Figure 105). The opening is cut into the main volume of the house below what appears to be the main floor. The lower portion of a door is visible through the partially screened opening. The implication is that this entrance leads to activities that are not appropriate for viewing by the public and that certainly are not related to the front door of a house.

Examined in greater detail, both houses now appear to be versions of another residential type, the one-and-a-half-story dwelling. A particularly modest variation of the earliest New England houses, this type lacks the iconic clarity of its predecessor but has the awkward charm of true folk houses, where utility was considered to be more important than form or style. The entrances on the gable ends distinguish the plans of these houses from the earliest houses of New England, which had their primary door on the eave facade and possessed central hearths.

The gable-fronted house (Figure 108), introduced by the Greek Revival in the first half of the nineteenth century in imitation of the pediment of a Greek temple, allowed for a narrower lot in areas where speculation made higher land utilization desirable. Later, in resort areas, cottages were placed in close adjacency to minimize expensive water frontage. Becoming the dominant vernacular house type in New England, gable-fronted houses forced drastic changes in planning. The replacement of fireplaces with wood-burning stoves removed the massive central hearth and allowed for more flexible plans.

A cottage type that became prevalent on Nantucket had porches facing the water and a gable-end entry on the street (Figures 109, 110). It is related to the storage buildings that were densely packed along the harbor waterways. The identical vocabularies of these two building types diminished the tradi-

104. Cape Cod Style house, Gibson County, Indiana, circa 1935.   105. Venturi and Rauch, Trubek House, Nantucket Island, Massachusetts, 1970–71. Elevations.   106. Venturi and Rauch, Trubek House, Nantucket Island, Massachusetts, 1970–71. Plans and sections.   107. Venturi and Rauch, Wislocki House, Nantucket Island, Massachusetts, 1970–71. Elevations, plans, and section.

104

105

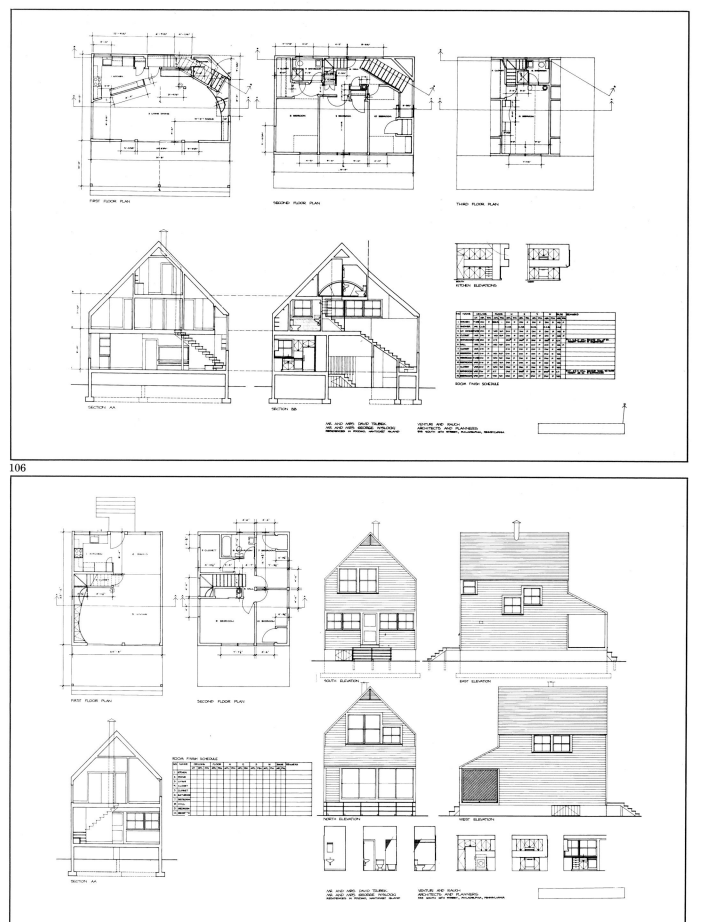

106

107

108

110

111

tional separation in imagery between house and shed to the point that they became indistinguishable. The fishing shacks on Nantucket (Figure 111), first built in the seventeenth century as temporary dwellings, offer another local vernacular tradition that uses the same materials and detailing as the later sheds along the harbor. This tradition of modest structures suggests a kind of heroic poverty that is in keeping with the sensibility of both the first houses of New England and the Venturi houses.

The Jethro Coffin House of 1686 (Figure 112), supposedly the oldest house on Nantucket, has the same regular shingle wall and roof treatment as the Trubek and Wislocki Houses. The rake is finished with a simple board and there is minimal eave detailing. The equally minimal casings around the windows and doors of the Venturi houses suggest the timbered surrounds of the Jethro Coffin House. The gable end of the Coffin House has the random distribution of openings of varying sizes that is common to saltbox houses and Cape Cod cottages and that would become an integral part of the later Nantucket vernacular that leads to the Venturi houses. Yet the scale of the openings on those two houses (Figures 105, 107) is drastically altered from the historical precedent. Oversized double-hung window sashes occupy the facades in an apparently random manner. Position and size are not held constant on the facades of either house. The window sashes are divided vertically down their center to form a cross with the horizontal member. The scale is completely different from the tiny panes of the earliest Nantucket houses or the later replacement sash of the local vernacular. Scale is further questioned by the positioning of windows that touch eave boards and corner trim. Similar groupings of windows are encountered, however, in the storage sheds and cottages of Nantucket (Figure 110) to suggest once more that the Venturi houses are governed by rules of a util-

108. Gable Front house, Hussey Street, Nantucket, Nantucket Island, Massachusetts, early nineteenth century. 109. Loft houses, Old North Wharf, Nantucket, Nantucket Island, Massachusetts, 1850s. Waterfront facades. 110. Loft houses, Old North Wharf, Nantucket, Nantucket Island, Massachusetts, 1850s. Street facades. 111. "Auld Lang Syne," Siasconset, Nantucket Island, Massachusetts, 1675.

itarian origin. In fact, the size of the sash in relation to the field of the facade gives to the entire structure a sense of drastic miniaturization, as though the facade had been shrunk in size but the openings had retained their normative size and now crowd the facade. The two dwellings resemble secondary buildings which, like outbuildings on an estate, are generally found in the company of more impressive structures.

The Trubek House south facade is dominated by a grouping of windows that approximates a Palladian window (Figure 105). Its proportions, however, have been severely compressed along the vertical axis, and the overall symmetry has been disrupted by the insertion of a blank panel and by a horizontal slippage of the vertical members. The use of strip windows is a familiar device in medieval buildings and is one of the primary compositional elements of modern architecture, but their conjunction with a Palladian window creates the impression that the Trubek facade has its origins in an extremely compressed form of the Shingle Style. Closer examination reveals that a toilet and lavatory are visible in one half of the arched lunette of the Palladian window (Section BB in Figure 106)—indicating a floor level in an unanticipated location and suggesting an interior complexity that had not been expected. It also implies a highly eccentric use of traditional elements, since the other half of the arched opening obviously belongs to another spatial unit.

The fenestration of Wislocki House south facade also includes horizontal strip windows (Figure 107). Broken in the middle by the door, this opening extends the full width to divide the facade panel into two distinct regions and destroy the continuity of solid surface. This is a device frequently encountered in modern architecture but is also possible in the Shingle Style. The back porches of New England farmhouses that are glazed in winter with storm windows closely resemble this arrangement. In both houses, the interior partitioning behind the window sashes allows views through the entire structure to suggest that the houses contain rooms that are much larger than is expected from the evidence of the volumes and fenestration.

The Wislocki House is the simpler and in many ways more inviting house to examine in the round (Figure 107). Circling

112. Jethro Coffin House, Nantucket, Nantucket Island, Massachusetts, 1686.

113

the house in a path that leads first between the two structures, one sees a tiny window in the upper left corner of the east elevation. Pressed under the eave, this window is pushed to the limits of the facade with a modern abstract sensibility to suggest that a corner space of no significance lies behind it. In the center of the facade, two identical windows are slipped vertically along a center piece of trim—an arrangement that normally indicates the change in floor level associated with the placement of an interior stair. Kitchen and toilet exhaust hoods and a plumbing vent appear in the random positions dictated by necessity; they are secondary features of an entirely utilitarian nature.

The porch projecting from the end of this elevation is clearly an additive structural unit, even though the concrete block foundation continues under the porch rather than turning to follow the north face of the house. Quite common in nineteenth-century urban dwellings, such a raised foundation is not found in early New England houses and is only rarely encountered in the Nantucket cottages, which are more often raised on piles. The raised foundation creates both storage space and the solid podium that gives the house an added monumentality. The effect is reminiscent of small structures of ritual significance. The supports as well as the railing details of the porch are built with oversized lumber sections. Similar in detail to the piers, fences, and porches of Nantucket, and drawn from that tradition, they question the scale of the entire structure.

On the gable-end, north elevation facing the water, stairs extend the entire length of the porch with two continuous treads that form a monumental approach as well as function as a continuous bench. Two large openings separated by a single structural support are cut into the house. Each opening has a pair of sliding glass doors. These doors make no attempt to deny their modern origin and satisfy the desire to optimize access to the water. The symmetry of the lower, porch half of the facade is disrupted by a narrow, shingled panel to suggest either a functional change or the presence of an object behind the panel that would prohibit a fully glazed wall. The second asymmetrical element is the latticed screen at one end of the porch, which blocks the view to the adjoining property. Such lattices were commonly used to screen Shingle Style porches and are also a familiar element on the fishermen's houses in

the Nantucket Island village of Siasconset (Figure 113).

Stepping in from the overhang of the porch roof, the windows of the upper facade imply a functional arrangement that reflects the needs of the spaces behind them. An overscaled, double-hung sash is directly adjacent to a sash of a more normal scale but which preserves approximately the proportions of the larger window. This arrangement of windows apparently represents a major chamber that is joined at its side by a minor chamber; the two rooms seem to extend the full width of the gable. A vent at the apex of the rake angle substantiates the suggested presence of two bedrooms which, pressed up against the inner slope of the roof, face the sea. This is common to Nantucket cottages.

On the outboard, west facade of the Wislocki House, are found an identical pair of windows that duplicate the smaller, upstairs window on the ocean facade. They suggest the existence of either one long, thin room extending the length of the house or two small chambers of equal size divided by a partition that dies into the central mullion—a modern convention of division. The latter possibility seems to be more plausible in terms of the function of the structure. The only other opening in this facade is a storage hatch in the foundation wall.

Completing the circuit around the house, and remembering the information gained on the other three sides, one is able to understand the apparently primary, south entrance facade. The door that opens to the road is used for entry. But, judging from the evidence of the major openings on the north, ocean facade, the minor spaces of the house fall behind this south facade. As is common in vernacular building and ordinary suburban homes, primary access is forced through the kitchen door to the kitchen and eating area that lie behind the strip windows. The second-floor double-sash window is harder to analyze since it is identical to the paired sash on the ocean facade that apparently opens into a major bedroom. The blinds, indicating both a functional change and a partition behind the central mullion, give a clue.

113. Wade property, Siasconset, Nantucket Island, Massachusetts, 1789.   114. Parson Capen House, Topsfield, Massachusetts, 1683. Staircase.   115. Reconstruction of Henry David Thoreau's Hut, Walden Pond, Massachusetts, originally built in 1845.

114

115

117

Blinds that pull down are used in all the bedroom windows. A blind that pulls up would indicate a combined need for light and additional privacy during daytime use. The presence of a plumbing vent confirms the suspicion that a bathroom must lie behind the right sash.

The primitive joinery and brute scale of the stairs leading up to the door resemble closely the detailing of the Nantucket docks and piers. The railings die into the siding without any transition or trim. The light above the door is a common exterior, waterproof fixture of the most ordinary design. The screen door is reminiscent of those found in farm kitchens. The door itself resembles the earliest paneled doors in New England houses where the use of only two panels gave to the door an overscaled feeling when compared to more conventional, multipaneled doors.

As suggested by the external arrangement, the door opens between the kitchen and the dining area. The space flows toward the large, sliding glass doors that open to the porch and the sea. The kitchen on the east side is shielded from the living area beyond by the stair volume; full-height appliances and storage back into the supporting wall of the stair while a coat closet, in a location characteristic of many folk dwellings, opens under the stair. The sink faces, in a conventional manner, the window that looks toward the access path.

The placement of the entry, service, and major living areas, ending with the porch and its view, resembles the spatial configuration of a contemporary hotel or motel room. The walls are painted drywall and have the minimal trim of a constructional rather than decorative origin. A bench extending along the east wall from the stair volume to the sliding glass doors explains the offset opening in the north facade, which was shifted to avoid a conflict with the bench. The focus of the room is a laterally centered stove with a flue rising straight to the ceiling. The stair, starting its ascent on treads cut into the bench and rising on winders to slip between its supporting walls, doubles back behind the stove. The result is reminiscent of the cramped

and sharply rising stairs that are squeezed behind the fireplace in Colonial houses to minimize their intrusion into precious living space (Figure 114). The slipped window on the east facade lights the stair from above.

The stair rises steeply, cutting into the space of the upper hall, so that upon arrival at the second floor, the doors to the two minor bedrooms on the west side confront the void of the stairwell in an abrupt manner. Again, the tight space and minimal dimensions suggest the most economical of utilitarian structures. To the right at the head of the stairs, the door to the main bedroom is skewed to allow for access to the neighboring minor bedroom. The exterior reading of the fenestration proves to be accurate, for two symmetrical chambers do extend the length of the west side of the house and the main chamber is lit by the large window above the porch. The windows, oversized on the exterior, are even more dramatic when seen from the compressed spaces of the interior. The bathroom, as suspected, is located over the kitchen door and is lit by the sash with the atypical blind that draws up. A storage room, lit by the least significant window in the house, occupies the southeast corner of the building.

The exterior hierarchy of window and door types allows one to read the Wislocki House simply, without clues other than size and position. The entire building can be interpreted as a coherent organization of pragmatic concerns and the logical expression of elements. Using neither applied ornament nor significant figurative pieces, it resembles the best of New England architecture which was formed by usage into an eloquent object. Complexity appears only in those passages of the building where actual difficulties occur in resolving the conflicting dimensional requirements between necessary functional elements. In this sense, the building satisfies the criteria of orthodox modern architecture and is a logical extension of the New England traditions.

In *Complexity and Contradiction in Architecture* (1966), Venturi traces the argument of New England, extending from Horatio Greenough to Henry David Thoreau and finally emerging as a principle in the words of Louis Sullivan, that form follows function. Certainly the hut built by Thoreau at Walden Pond (Figure 115) could be seen as the ancestor to the Wislocki House. But, in this house, Venturi turns the logic of New

116. *Balch House, Beverly, Massachusetts, seventeenth century. Attic chamber.* 117. *Story House, Essex, Massachusetts, circa 1684. Hall, as installed in the Henry Francis du Pont Winterthur Museum.*

118

England architecture against its own traditional forms. The sensual quality of heavy timber construction, aged wood surfaces and romantically lit attic chambers is gone (Figure 116). Also gone is the massive and reassuring central chimney block with the family fire flickering on the hearth (Figure 117). The Wislocki House is a light, balloon-frame structure built of two by fours with thin partitions clad in taped and painted drywall. Necessary utilitarian objects, modern mechanical and electrical systems, are displayed without embarrassment. Only a faint residual aroma of the beloved houses of New England is left. In their place stands a house that is built with the same tough-minded objectivity of the original carpenters of New England.

The dramatization of the diminution in scale of the Wislocki House is accomplished through the use of standard, double-hung sash whose oversized panes of glass seem particularly brutal in the context of historic New England buildings. This device makes us realize that the expectations of today are drastically different from those of the past. We live in a diminished world that no longer allows for the extravagance of massive materials and the fine handwork of skilled craftsmen. The vernacular tradition is gone. It can still be tapped to breathe life into our houses, but sentimentality and the imitation of drained ornamental forms must be avoided in order to produce an architecture of true significance.

The adjacent Trubek House (Figure 105) suggests an extension to this argument. Perhaps the pursuit of modesty and utility that is found in the Wislocki House, and is a continuing tradition in New England, is not enough to be fully representative or expressive of today's world. Perhaps the objective simplicity of the Wislocki House denies the complexity and potential richness of the present. Though the Trubek House, when seen from afar, displays the language and detailing of the Wislocki House, closer examination reveals some notable exceptions to their apparent similarity.

The south elevation of the Trubek House, toward the access drive, is dominated by the oversized and slightly deformed Palladian window. The southwest corner of the facade has been cut in a manner associated with the Shingle Style. While the absence of a symmetrical response on the other corner of the facade negates the expected sense of verticality and uplift, this cut articulates the gable as a pure triangle. The relationship of

cut to gable recalls the Old Windmill of 1746 (Figure 118) on Nantucket Island, whose octagonal base similarly isolates the roof volume.

The insertion of a floor between the lunette and the lower strip windows of the Palladian window questions the assumption that the house is a two-story structure like its companion. Whether there are three floors, or only two with an oversized ground floor, remains ambiguous. The opening below, leading to a stair behind the screen, is also puzzling—its width suggests a major entrance; its screening indicates a more utilitarian point of access. A cutout pattern of slots, the screen both duplicates a technique used in folk architecture to represent economically a figure in profile and acts as a miniature representation of the Nantucket picket fence, which has been pressed into the facade to retain the intensity of the object quality of the house.

The west elevation of the Trubek House is also deformed by the diagonal cut at its southwest corner. The single large window abutting the trim of the house allows for a double reading of either a void pressed against the edge of a square panel or, if the diagonal cut is discounted, a void centered on the facade. The window has fixed panes but maintains the language of the double-hung sash. The size of this opening, the largest in either house, gives it an iconic property of great power. Viewed from this side, the house at first appears to be a single-cell structure with a porch. Through the immense opening can be seen a second plane with a window of a more normal scale. The impression gained from this detail is that the house was built as a single volume and was then subdivided in such a way that the interior spaces interact with the preexisting system of fenestration in an erratic manner.

The porch, although apparently quite simple and similar to the one on the Wislocki House, is actually a strange hybrid between an attached structure and a carved-out volume. Half embedded, half attached, it combines the characteristics of two, typically American solutions while denying them both. Extending across the north, ocean facade, the porch differs from the Wislocki House porch in its use of three posts instead of two: the center post bisects a symmetrical void to create a compositional duality. As in the Wislocki House, ordinary sliding aluminum doors open into the major space of the living area. A band of stairs stretches across the base of the entire porch.

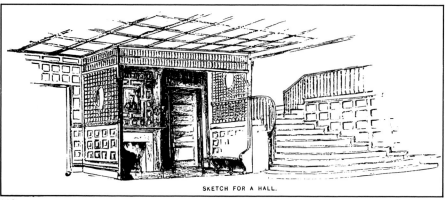

SKETCH FOR A HALL.

119

The second-floor fenestration above the porch is a band of sashes that implies modern strip windows; they are capped by a pair of similar windows to reveal the presence of a third floor. Their arrangement suggests a series of bedrooms of equal size on the second floor with an attic room lodged above them. The end result is a quite ordinary facade that is reminiscent of nineteenth-century urban, vernacular housing.

The east facade is straightforward in its choice of elements but intriguing in their arrangement. An oversized pair of sashes adjoins the void of the porch yet avoids horizontal alignment at their head. Above these, a second pair of smaller windows press up under the eave and slide forward over the void of the porch to emphasize the awkwardness of the porch connection and to question the exact location of the floor. The storage hatch opening into the foundation has no apparent geometric relationship with the other elements of the facade.

To reach the south, entrance facade, one must approach the house diagonally from the parking area on a path perpendicular to the chamfered corner of the Trubek House. This corner plane acquires a frontality that reduces the actual facades to secondary planes and confronts the access route in a way that gives to the structure an added formidability. Though one is drawn onward to the south facade by the Palladian window, the screened nature and dropped position of the opening below question the possibility of entrance. The view of the silhouette of the porch makes this entrance all the more ambiguous. Approaching obliquely, the path slides under the facade into a narrow zone of exterior space that ascends behind the screen up a half-flight of stairs. A modern, horizontal window within the entrance porch opens a view into the living space. The stair, establishing a circulation zone parallel to the face of the building, climbs to a door at the approximate center of the house.

Through this entrance door, the space flows from a rear wall warped into the configuration of a shallow apse toward the porch and the water (Figure 106). The kitchen is screened, and is pressed back into the southeast corner behind the living

area. From the opposite corner, a stair winds back overhead to rise over the door into the shallow zone defined by the entrance stair below. A bench, carved away in semicircular treads to provide a base for the stair, runs intermittently from the entrance window, along the west wall, to the porch. The treading is similar to that of the bench in the Wislocki House, but the result is more reminiscent of the large stair halls in Shingle Style houses, where benches and platforms were frequently used to begin stairs at ground level (Figure 119). A single, square column which stands free in the space suggests an ancestry in either Cubist plans or early Le Corbusier (Figure 120), or possibly even in the compositional virtuosity of Alvar Aalto. The oversized window in the east facade, illuminating the dining area, creates a diagonal spatial flow across the room from the dining area to the window above the stair and subverts the original, simple understanding of the living space as an apsed megaron.

The stair rises into a slot between the enormous window in the west facade and the interior window wall behind it. The stair volume crosses the corner of the room at a thirty-degree angle—more obliquely than the forty-five-degree angle of the chamfered corner it follows. Reaching the zone over the entrance, the stair is bathed in light from the strip windows which form the lower portion of the Palladian window. This contradicts the language developed in the Wislocki House, where rows of double-hung sash illuminate small rooms of similar scale and use. At the top, the stair collides with a wall to reduce the clear passage to a dimension that will continue up the attic stair.

The upstairs hall is a residual space bounded by doors of varying sizes. The symmetry of the north elevation is reflected in the straightforward layout of three, ocean-facing bedrooms, yet each room deforms its rectilinear disposition with a projecting intrusion while the two outboard rooms rise volumetrically into the attic space to further the discrepancy between interior space and exterior volume. Reversing the expected and traditional treatments of primary and secondary spaces, and resembling elements of the early houses of Le Corbusier, the bathroom is the only regular geometric volume on the interior.

From the second-floor hallway, a door opens into the stair

118. *Old Windmill, Nantucket, Nantucket Island, Massachusetts, 1746. 119. Henry Hobson Richardson, Sketch for a Hall, n.d.*

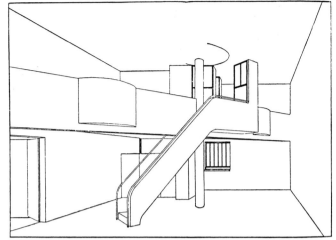

120   121

that leads to the attic room. Smaller and even more labyrinthine than the primary stair, this stair rises into a space illuminated by one half of the lunette window and turns at right angles to enter the central attic room that is pressed up into the apex of the roof volume. A view of the sea is framed by two, symmetrically placed windows in the north wall, but the centrality and figural symmetry of the space is challenged by the asymmetrical placement of storage units and the stair entrance. The stove pipe rising from the living area intrudes into this space and angles along the roof intrados to exit at the same position below the ridge beam as the flue in the Wislocki House.

The Trubek House takes the argument of the Wislocki House—that architecture be driven by program and logical construction—and subverts the constructional imperative while retaining the celebration of usage through complex patterns of circulation. One is reminded of the early houses of Le Corbusier and Aalto where the dramatization of passage was accompanied by unexpected lighting. The development of an open living area that has neither a particular shape nor any geometric clarity but is instead a spatial flow continuously modulated by the placement of secondary elements is common to both high modern architecture (Figure 121) and the Trubek House. The bedrooms on the second floor are simply arranged and the circulation spaces on the upper levels continue the open, flowing sensibility of the living area. The entire structure is animated by a circulation pattern that assumes a life of its own as it traverses the volume of the house.

Yet this intense convolution of passage occurs, not within the simple cubic volume proposed by Le Corbusier, but in a dwelling shape that is recognizably and particularly American (Figure 105). The language of the exterior belies the spatial complexity of the interior, where the lack of historical detail avoids the problem of an architecture based on sentiment. On the exterior, the strange Palladian window is the most insistently historical and figural element. Originating in Renaissance and Mannerist architecture, this element became a key motif in English Palladian and Georgian architecture. Introduced into

America as a detail of Georgian Colonial architecture, it was borrowed again by the Shingle Style (Figure 103). Frank Lloyd Wright took it over for his own house of 1889 in Oak Park, Illinois (Figure 13) but erased the historical associations by eventually removing the lunette. In the Trubek House, this same motif is contorted into an emblem of the thought process of the house. It becomes ambiguous and stylistically imprecise—in a sense, it is subsumed by the vernacular.

This house, like the Wislocki House, maintains the toughness and austerity that are so poignant in American terms. Enough of the vernacular is preserved to release a chain of associations familiar to any American. But the virtuosity of a spatial manipulation associated with heroic Modernism is introduced to enrich the house inestimably. The abstract, artistic complexity of arrangement can be appreciated in a direct and purely visual way. The masterly use of light adds an experimental quality that should be apparent to every visitor. Finally, the dialogue between interior and exterior argues that we live in a period after an immediate past that produced an architecture of an abstract brilliance. That architecture had no place for representational associations and closed forever the door to the more distant past. Yet the dialogue with our complete past, with all its richness and memories, should continue. Out of this dialogue, we can once more recover our heritage without resorting to dry, academic reconstructions. Vernacular architecture opens a source that can embrace all of the imperatives that have driven architecture for the last one hundred years. It offers an expressive range of vast dimension; it is ours, we created it and we should protect it through reinterpretation of its treasures for future generations. Together, the Trubek and Wislocki Houses offer an alternative to Laugier's primitive hut, an alternate model that is peculiarly and particularly American.

---

120. Le Corbusier, Houses in a Series for Artisans project, 1924. Plan.   121. Le Corbusier, Houses in a Series for Artisans project, 1924. Interior perspective.

The Image in the Empty Frame: Wu Hall and the Art of Representation

Stephen Kieran, Princeton University

Michael Baxandall, in *Painting and Experience in Fifteenth Century Italy* (1972), presents and analyzes conventional meanings ascribed to hand gestures in fifteenth-century Florentine art (Figure 122). He demonstrates that members of the Florentine community agreed as a society to the meanings of various gestures, and that these conventions gave members of that community access to and understanding of paintings produced by other members of the community. Massacio's fresco, *The Expulsion from Paradise* (Figure 123), is an example that Baxandall holds up for analysis of its gestural conventions.

Abstracting the gestures in the Massaco fresco into a contemporary context, I suspect most of us would consider such modes of expression to be mere histrionics—an emotional display for a theatrical, and therefore insincere, purpose. The ancient sense of the word *rhetoric* as the study of rules of composition and the art of effective speech and writing, has fallen into disuse. The word today has largely assumed a single meaning: the display of form without substance.

This essay will examine a single building by Venturi, Rauch and Scott Brown, Gordon Wu Hall of 1980–83 at Princeton University (Plate 7 and Figure 124), as an essay in the *substantive* rhetoric of architectural convention—both *constructive* and *historic*. The external spatial context and internal form of Wu Hall will not be considered in detail, as these have been well presented elsewhere.[1] I will also use Wu Hall to demonstrate the close correspondence between the theories presented some fifteen years earlier in Robert Venturi's *Complexity and Contradiction in Architecture* (1966) and the form of this building itself.

In his introduction to *Complexity and Contradiction in Architecture*, Vincent Scully had the foresight to predict that this new work would form the opposite pole across history to Le Corbusier's 1923 polemic, *Vers une architecture*. A consideration of the stances Le Corbusier and Robert Venturi take toward conventional form in these two works reveals the accuracy of this twenty-year-old prediction. Despite the fact that some recent work, such as that of Leon Krier and Allan Greenberg, may push the historic pole even further from Le Corbusier toward this dimension of conventional representation, *Complexity and Contradiction* continues to exist as a bellwether of modern theory and practice. For Le Corbusier, purist art theory provided the basis for his attitudes toward conventions, architectural and otherwise.[2] New, improved versions of houses, machines, and articles of everyday use were to replace their predecessors. By a process of continuous discard and reconstruction, all cultural artifacts were to evolve toward their ultimate conventional form as fixed object-types: perfected machines—be they houses, cars, or briar pipes. The goal of scrapping was to reduce artifacts to their simplest common denominator. An analogy to engineering practice, with its continuous and empirical testing, rejection, and updated reconstruction, provided the model discipline for Le Corbusier's vision of the object-type.

Like Le Corbusier, Robert Venturi builds his theory in *Complexity and Contradiction* upon a belief in conventional form. Also like Le Corbusier, he holds to a conviction in the progressive development of cultural artifacts as new technologies and programmatic concerns subject existing conventions to reevaluation. Here, however, Venturi parts way with his forefather and moves to another pole of history. In *Complexity and Contradiction*, Venturi states:

Conventional elements in architecture represent one stage in an evolutionary development, and they contain in their changed use and expression some of their past as well as their new meaning. What can be called the vestigial element parallels the double-functioning element. It is distinct from a superfluous element because it contains a double meaning. This is the result of a more or less ambiguous combination of the old meaning, called up by associations, with a new meaning created by the modified or new function, structural or programmatic, and the new context.[3]

Venturi's process of making conventions assumes, unlike Le Corbusier's scrapheap of discarded culture, a historical dimension. Succeeding artifacts are to contain aspects of their predecessors within the new form. If the term did not have perjorative connotations, one could describe this mode of convention-forming as almost cannibalistic (indeed Le Corbusier would have described it so); vestiges of previous forms are to continue their existence within the new form as a reminder of historical evolution and tradition within contemporary culture.

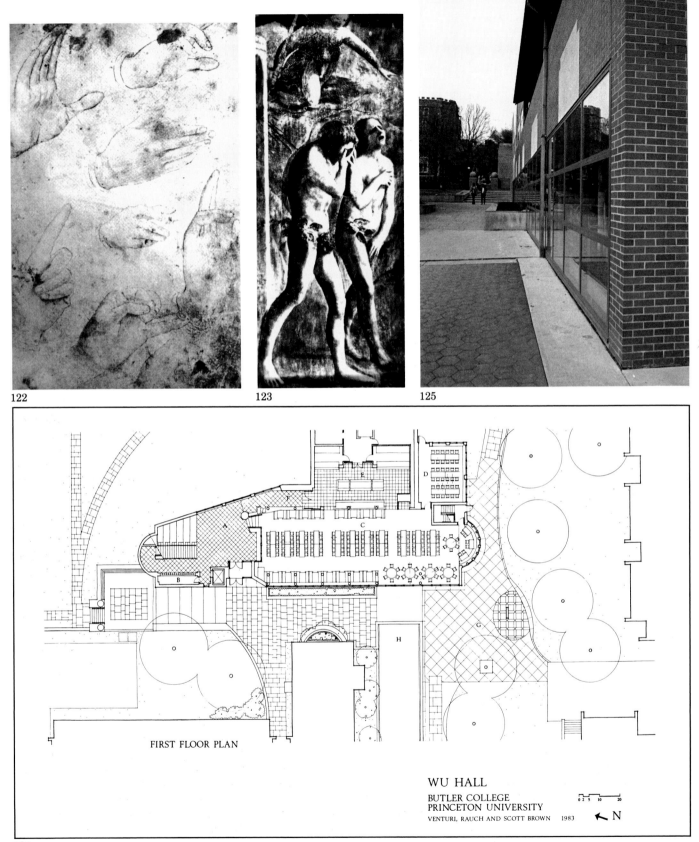

122

123

125

FIRST FLOOR PLAN

WU HALL

BUTLER COLLEGE
PRINCETON UNIVERSITY

VENTURI, RAUCH AND SCOTT BROWN   1983

N

124

126

While Le Corbusier's exemplar for the scrapping of past convention is the engineer, Venturi's role model for the retention of past form within new contexts is, of course, the great poet and rhetorician T. S. Eliot, who is widely quoted in *Complexity and Contradiction*. In fact, the theoretical structure and terminology used by Venturi in *Complexity and Contradiction* owe a great debt to Eliot and such literary critics as Cleanth Brooks.[4] The term *both-and*, for example, is borrowed from Cleanth Brooks. In the preface to *Complexity and Contradiction*, Venturi quotes at length T. S. Eliot's thought on the place of tradition in society:

Yet if the only form of tradition, of handing down, consisted in following the ways of the immediate generation before us in a blind or timid adherence to its successes, 'tradition' should be positively discouraged. . . .

Tradition is a matter of much wider significance. It cannot be inherited, and if you want it you must obtain it by great labour. It involves, in the first place, the historical sense . . . and the historical sense involves perception, not only of the pastness of the past, but of its presence; the historical sense compels a man to write not merely with his own generation in his bones, but with a feeling that the whole of the literature of Europe . . . has a simultaneous existence and composes a simultaneous order.

This historical sense, which is a sense of the timeless as well as the temporal and of the timeless and temporal together, is what makes a writer traditional, and it is at the same time what makes a writer most acutely conscious of his place in time, of his own

contemporaneity. . . . No poet, no artist of any kind, has complete meaning alone.[5]

Venturi relies upon Eliot not only for a general sense of the role of tradition in architecture, but also for specific rhetorical tactics (I use the word here in its classical sense) to embody the past within the present. For example, in *The Lovesong of J. Alfred Prufrock*, Eliot uses rhyme and position within a couplet to juxtapose the words *ices* and *crisis:* "Should I, after tea and cakes and ices, / Have the strength to force the moment to its crisis?"[6] The rhyme between "ices" and "crisis" demands that we compare the two lines. Juxtaposition heightens the discrepancy between the light-heartedness of the first line and the impending confrontation to follow. The conflicting emotions are made real and given presence by the use of the word *ices* to build the expectation of a frozen solid presence, while the rhyme with the word *crisis* in the line that follows undercuts this expectation with heated urgency. The emotions evoked by this juxtaposition are not simple. We empathize with the simultaneous presence of contrary desires to act and not to act.

While a poem is certainly not a building, both rely upon conventions for their meaning. It is the comparison of the conventional meanings and associations we as a society ascribe to the words *ices* and *crisis* that give Eliot's couplet its poignancy. Lessons in rhetoric such as this provided by Eliot have not been lost on Venturi.

The intention here is to show that Wu Hall is an inclusive essay in architectural convention. There is nothing especially technologically innovative about the building. Nor does it propose new forms. What Wu Hall does do, however, is—like Eliot's poem—force us to compare inconsistent, even irreconcilable conventions that have been improbably drawn together within the same constructive system. In confronting the building, we recognize the conventional forms and understand their associations. All architectural construction and form, both historic and contemporary, assumes a self-conscious sense of convention in this rhetorical world, with the improbable comparisons heightening our sense of both the past and present and proposing a world within which both coexist in an uneasy but meaningful juxtaposition.

122. Eight Studies of a Hand, *chalk and wash, mid-fifteenth-century Florentine.* 123. Massacio, The Expulsion from Paradise, *fresco, circa 1427. Santa Maria del Carmine, Florence.* 124. Venturi, Rauch and Scott Brown, Gordon Wu Hall, *Princeton University, Princeton, New Jersey, 1980–83. First-floor plan.* 125. Venturi, Rauch and Scott Brown, Gordon Wu Hall, *Princeton University, Princeton, New Jersey, 1980–83. Front facade from the south.* 126. William Le Baron Jenny, The Fair Building, Chicago, Illinois, 1891.

128

Consider first the long west wall of the building. Seen obliquely, it is absolutely flat, with brick, stone, and glazing in the same plane (Figure 125), while the windows unfold themselves across the base of the building in a continuous strip. The constructive convention for this type of building exterior is the curtain wall. It was made possible in the late nineteenth century by new, skeletal constructive systems in iron and concrete (Figure 126). The wall became simply a "skin" or enclosure designed to keep the elements out and to aid in the control of internal temperatures. Later developments in elastomeric sealants made it possible to place windows in the same plane as walls with the assurance that leakage would not occur.

Moving around to a perpendicular view of this elevation, two more features of the curtain wall system come into focus (Figure 127). First, one can clearly see the freestanding, round columns forming a structural frame behind the strip windows. One is reminded here of the Villa Savoie (Figure 128) with its columnar grid visible through windows and openings. Second, exposed expansion joints divide the brickwork into panels approximately fifteen feet in length in the conventional manner for brick curtain walls, and weep holes are located at the bottom of each panel. A view of the south wall of a contemporary hospital in Philadelphia illustrates the constructive conventions of this brick curtain wall building system with diagrammatic clarity (Figure 129). All the expected characteristics of a conventional curtain wall system thus display themselves along the length of Wu Hall's west elevation. Improbably inserted within this system, however, are five, large, incomplete representations or vestiges of keystones (Figure 130). They are improbable in that they are properly associated with a load-bearing masonry constructive system in which they conventionally occupy the center of an arched or flat opening with voussoirs or segmental stones to either side. In the Wu Hall keystone, the voussoirs are only hinted at by the notched top profile. Instead of the expected joints between stones, present in Hawksmoor's version at St. George-in-the-East (Figure 131), the stone is

127. Venturi, Rauch and Scott Brown, Gordon Wu Hall, Princeton University, Princeton, New Jersey, 1980–83. Detail of curtain wall.   128. Le Corbusier, Villa Savoie, Poissy, 1928–30.

127

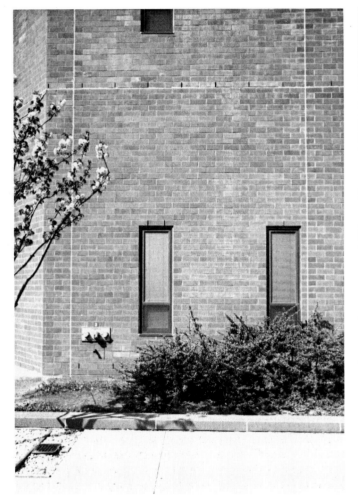

129   130

131

divided by an expansion joint. Not only are the Wu Hall keystones rendered incomplete by the absence of conventional, associated elements, but they are also cut off and left proportionately unfinished at the bottom. That is, their width suggests they should be much deeper; it is as though the curtain wall is literally just that—a curtain—a scrim laced with constructive conventions drawn from history rising to reveal the contemporary structural convention beyond (Figure 132). While one could say that it is the Modernist curtain wall strip window that here ironically undercuts the representation of traditional brick load-bearing construction, the relationship is much more subtle and rich than that interpretation suggests. Each modifies the perception of the other. Present construction exists but is rendered self-conscious by the inclusion of keystones as emblems of bearing wall construction. Although the keystones are rhetorical display, they perform an important function: they not only represent conventional, load-bearing masonry construction, but also force us to see contemporary curtain wall construction as a kind of convention in its own right.

Immediately to the north of the portion of wall we have just been considering is the building's gate-entry (Figure 133). The terms *gate* and *entry* are here coupled as a single hyphenated element because, like the portion of wall just examined, both associations exist simultaneously. Gate is a premodern concept. It implies ceremony—it celebrates the rite of passage. A gate emphatically separates inside from outside. Conversely, an entry minimizes the distinction between inside and outside. It is a simple functional passage, often through a glass wall detailed so as to minimize the distinction between inside and outside. With an entry, it is as though one passes through to the interior by osmosis rather than by conscious ritualistic passage—the biological metaphor here being more apt than the ritualistic one.

The gate-entry at Wu Hall combines both the premodern

129. Ballinger and Company, Graduate Hospital, University of Pennsylvania, Philadelphia, Pennsylvania, 1979. 130. Venturi, Rauch and Scott Brown, Gordon Wu Hall, Princeton University, Princeton, New Jersey, 1980–83. Detail of keystone. 131. Nicholas Hawksmoor, St. George-in-the-East, London, England, 1714–17. Aisle window.

132

and modern senses of passage. Although no exact single model exists, the general form of the gate evokes associations with Gothic portals elsewhere on the Princeton campus, which in turn draw upon English examples, especially at Oxford and Cambridge. On this general level, the quadripartite Wu Hall gate follows the Gothic model rather closely. At the base is the entry itself. Above the entry is a heraldic band surmounted by a bifurcated pair of windows. This bifurcation creates a duality that is resolved at the top by a second band of profiled heraldic emblems. A rather simple and small-scale version of such a portal exists on the Princeton campus at the north entrance to Holder Court (Figure 134). This portal consists of a pointed archway capped by a horizontal band of eight heraldic shields. A statue niche at the center heightens the duality created by the pair of windows above the heraldic band, and the whole composition is resolved by the pyramidal stepped profile of the cornice. Similar compositions exist at Weiboldt Hall (Figure 135) and Bartlett Gymnasium at the University of Chicago, and in numerous English scholastic examples (Figure 136).

Beyond these generic similarities to Gothic portals, the sources of Wu Hall's associative gate heraldry become quite diverse. The lower band between the portals and windows refers more closely to Renaissance and Neoclassical models than to Gothic ones. The arched niches recall such eighteenth-century entrance facades as St. Anthony's College (Figure 137), or a sixteenth-century design by Robert Smythson (Figure 138). The decorative rectangular panel with an inset circle is a motif common to many Renaissance decorative elements. It can be found repeatedly in Serlio's drawings of chimney pieces (Figure 139). It is just this sort of architectural element that Venturi was looking at and showing to the client, as a group of photographs from a presentation board shows (Figure 140).

The triangular and circular forms found in the panel above the windows are more explicitly Tudor than Gothic in origin. The triangular pediment and its accompanying panel below re-

132. Venturi, Rauch and Scott Brown, Gordon Wu Hall, Princeton University, Princeton, New Jersey, 1980–83. Front facade from the north toward Butler Plaza.   133. Venturi, Rauch and Scott Brown, Gordon Wu Hall, Princeton University, Princeton, New Jersey, 1980–83. Gate-entry.

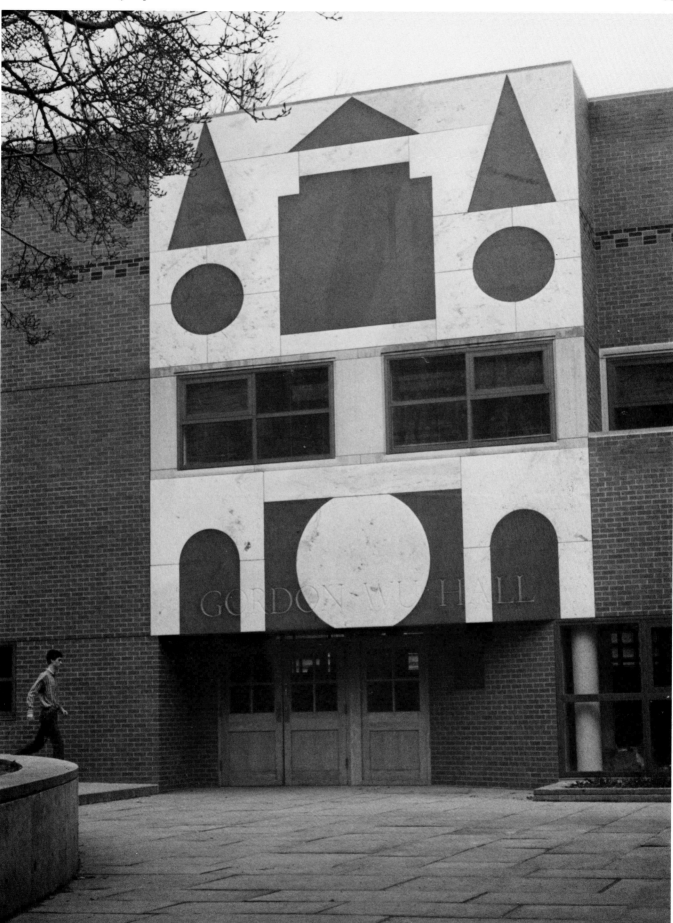

134

135

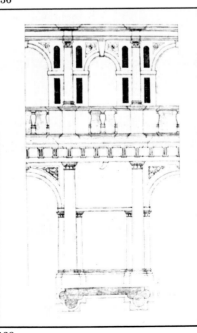

136

137

138

139

134. Day and Klauder, Holder Court, Princeton University, Princeton, New Jersey, 1917–19. Gate. 135. Collidge and Hodgdon, Weibolt Hall, University of Chicago, Chicago, Illinois, 1928. Gate. 136. John Fisher, St. John's College, Cambridge University, Cambridge, England, 1510–16. Main gate. 137. Charles Buckridge, St. Anthony's College, Oxford University, Oxford, England, 1780. 138. Robert Smythson, Design, probably for a Hall Screen, Nottinghamshire, England, 1586. 139. Sebastiano Serlio, Doric Chimneypiece, woodcut from Serlio, The Five Books of Architecture, *Venice, 1537. 140. Venturi, Rauch and Scott Brown, Presentation Board of Chimneypieces and Building Gates for Gordon Wu Hall, 1980.*

140

141

142

143

call such cornice pieces as that of the Fellows Quadrangle Gate at Oxford (Figure 141), or the University Examination Schools by Thomas Jackson (Figure 142). Elizabethan pedimented cornices also evoke imagery comparable to that of the Wu Hall portal. The decorative cornicepiece atop the end bay of the New Exchange in the Strand (Figure 143) is just the sort of antecedent that the Wu Hall portal top recalls. The New Exchange has a freestanding pedimented top above a rectangular window, flanked on both sides by pinnacles atop rounded urns. Wu Hall is a flattened, abstract version of this type of cornicepiece. The gable end decorative panel at Kirby Hall, Northamptonshire (Figure 144), with its recessed circular panel surmounted by an obelisk, as well as the garden pavilion cornice decorations at Burghley House (Figure 145), are yet other points of reference for the Wu Hall portal. This last garden structure by Capability Brown displays the same obelisk-above-circle feature in outline form as Kirby Hall. Again, the presence of comparable building gates found in the panel of photographs from the Venturi, Rauch and Scott Brown office at the time confirms the role these models played in the Wu Hall portal design (Figure 140).

The point of this rather exhaustive search for the pedigree of the Wu Hall portal heraldry is to portray the portal for what it is: an eclectic, historically organized dictionary of gate motifs. While the reference of the overall form is to a Gothic gate type found elsewhere in the Collegiate Gothic architecture of Princeton, as well as in English scholastic architecture, one has to search creatively through the history of English and American architecture for the specific associations of its details. No single model reveals all. While the circle-within-rectangle motif and the semicircular arched niches of the lower panel generally recall the classical tradition through specific references re-

144   145

141. John Akroyd and John Bentley under Warden Savile, Fellow's Quadrangle Gate, Merton College, Oxford University, Oxford, England, 1609–1610. 142. Thomas Jackson, University Examination Schools, Oxford, England, 1882. 143. Robert Smythson, The New Exchange in the Strand, London, England, 1609. 144. Robert Smythson, Kirby Hall, Northamptonshire, England, 1570–73. Gable. 145. Capability Brown, Garden Pavilion, Burghley House, Northamptonshire, England, 1760.

148

146

spectively to late Renaissance, Serlian chimneypieces and to eighteenth-century Neoclassical portals, the heraldry of the top panel connects itself to the late sixteenth- and early seventeenth-century work of Smythson and others, as well as its later eighteenth-century reflowering in the hands of Capability Brown. The breadth of the references Venturi evokes here is substantial. The Wu Hall portal compels one to search out and consider anew the relevance not of *a* tradition, but of *many* traditions. It asks us to remember the entire tradition of English learning embodied in Oxford and Cambridge. It alludes to both the classical and Gothic traditions of those institutions. It asks us to accept not only the early flowerings of those two great traditions, classical and Gothic, but also their subsequent revivals. The flat stone panels stare blankly out at us, representing the simultaneous validity and equality not only of Serlio, the Renaissance chronicler transported to Elizabethan soil, but also of the later Neoclassical models. Similarly, we witness the flattening of both Smythson's Elizabethan forms and Capability Brown's later Gothic Revival versions into abstract stone panels. While the early version of a form or language is not forgotten, Venturi does not let a search for origins obscure important later contributions. He is, by his own admission, fascinated as much by Day and Klauder's machined, stylized renditions of Gothic tracery (Figure 146), as by the real thing in the Gothic cathedrals of England, France, and Germany.

While all these references establish the Wu Hall portal as "gate," Venturi is equally preoccupied with its modernity as "entry." Heraldry aside, the actual point of passage into the building is more entry than gate (Figure 147). It is an undercut curtain wall more reminiscent of Aalto (Figure 148) than of Smythson. One enters under the building rather than into it. Reinforcing this modernist reading, the doors are not positioned symmetrically relative to the other elements of the facade (Figure 133), and a brick panel to the right of the doors

146. Day and Klauder, Rockefeller College Dining Hall (formerly Madison Hall), Princeton University, Princeton, New Jersey, 1917–19. Entrance.   147. Venturi, Rauch and Scott Brown, Gordon Wu Hall, Princeton University, Princeton, New Jersey, 1980–83. Entrance.   148. Alvar Aalto, Scandinavia Bank, Helsinki, Finland, 1962.

149

151

is inflected at an angle to the facade. The chief indication of entry here is the deep-set shadow pocket at the base of the building. The way into the building is simply a passing-through.

In an earlier comparison, the long facade was likened to a stage curtain laced with historical forms rising part way to present a glimpse of the Modernist structure that lies beyond (Figure 132). This curtain extends past the strip windows to include the entry as well (Figure 149). Just as the keystones are cut off and rendered incomplete by the horizontal strip windows, so too is the heraldic form of the gate left unfinished and undercut by the entry. Proportionately, one would expect the niches to be deeper than they are. It is as though the heraldic gate has been pried up and the entry slid beneath it. An exposed steel lintel spans the entry beneath the screen, reinforcing the juxtaposition of Modernist entry to historicist gate (Figure 150). The historical associations are consistently undercut by contemporary forms and construction. The quality of the heraldic gate as a two-dimensional screen is reinforced from below by the demonstration of the screen's thinness as it passes down over the entry, and from the south side by the exposed marble veneer to display the thinness of the wall.

Similarly, the insertion of horizontal, flush, strip windows between the bottom and top heraldic panels again juxtaposes modern construction and past form (Figure 133). While the color of these window frames is a Gothic-like lead grey and the window surrounds are limestone, the references to Collegiate Gothic windows stop there (Figure 151). In both their horizontal proportions and their flatness, they are thoroughly modern.

Even in a small detail, such as the lintel to a secondary egress door from the private dining room (Figure 152), one finds the

150

149. Venturi, Rauch and Scott Brown, Gordon Wu Hall, Princeton University, Princeton, New Jersey, 1980–83. Sketch of gate-entry by Robert Venturi, 1981. 150. Venturi, Rauch and Scott Brown, Gordon Wu Hall, Princeton University, Princeton, New Jersey, 1980–83. Steel lintel over entrance. 151. Day and Klauder, Holder Hall, Princeton University, Princeton, New Jersey, 1917–19. Window. 152. Venturi, Rauch and Scott Brown, Gordon Wu Hall, Princeton University, Princeton, New Jersey, 1980–83. Door to private dining room.

154

same insistence on the simultaneous presence of matter-of-fact contemporary construction and historical form. The presence of Gothic-like limestone window surrounds to the right of the door recalls a more historically correct approach, albeit with significantly altered proportions. Although Venturi could have carried the limestone lintel over the door to the left, he chose instead to leave it incomplete. The small rectangular piece of limestone at the intersection of the door and window is the vestige of a stone lintel over the door, rendered rhetorical by the explicit presence of a steel lintel. It is the presence of this vestigial, incomplete stone lintel, however, that draws one's attention to the purpose and presence of the steel lintel. Rhetorical display here strengthens our perception of contemporary constructive reality, and contemporary constructive reality is in turn rendered rhetorical by the historical presence of the vestigial stone lintel.

The great round bay windows at both the north and south ends of the building perform a double function (Figures 153, 154). On the one hand, they are two-story monitors that flood the ends of the building with light and cut the second floor of the building loose within the building volume—reinforcing the modernity of its construction (Figure 155). At the same time, they are emblematic of Elizabethan Hall bay windows as well as of the late nineteenth- and early twentieth-century reappearance of the multistory bay window in the works of Lutyens, Mackintosh, and others. As a plan prototype, great bay windows, both round and multisided, were often used by Robert Smythson as the termini to his end elevations. Burton Agnes Hall (Figure 156) is an example of the apsidal bay window appearing on the gable end of an Elizabethan building. The shape of the bay is rounded like the end bays at Wu Hall, but the space contained behind the bay is three, stacked, single stories. For a spatial prototype, one has to turn to the work of such late nineteenth- and early twentieth-century architects as Lutyens, who used a double volume bay window at Little

153. Venturi, Rauch and Scott Brown, Gordon Wu Hall, Princeton University, Princeton, New Jersey, 1980–83. North bay window. 154. Venturi, Rauch and Scott Brown, Gordon Wu Hall, Princeton University, Princeton, New Jersey, 1980–83. South bay window.

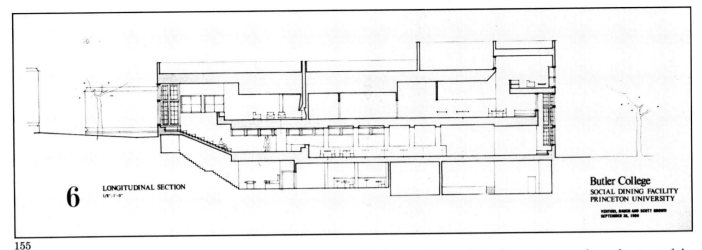

6 LONGITUDINAL SECTION
1/8" . 1'-0"

Butler College
SOCIAL DINING FACILITY
PRINCETON UNIVERSITY

VENTURI, RAUCH AND SCOTT BROWN
SEPTEMBER 26, 1980

155

Thakeham (Figure 157). The pattern, scale, and extent of the glazing in the Wu Hall bay windows are also generally evocative of Elizabethan glazing. A tripartite vertical division of bay window glazing is common to many Elizabethan buildings, such as Wootton Lodge (Figure 158). Generally, the English examples are characterized by the decreasing size of the stone subdivisions of the window. At their base, these bays are often four lites high, decreasing to three lites in the middle band and to two lites at the top. The effect of this particular set of subdivisions is to lighten the facade and to suggest a taller, narrower bay. Venturi follows this pattern in the north bay (Figure 153), but alters it in the south bay to a four-five-three rhythm of lites (Figure 154). This pattern, coupled with the exceptionally high parapet above and the low base combine to give the bay a rather squashed, almost submerged appearance. The association with Elizabethan bay windows, which often rose three or more very high stories, sharpens one's sense of the incompletion of this form. Like the flattened, low dining hall beyond, the bay as the external symbol of the great hall is also left dramatically submerged and incomplete at Wu Hall.

The insistence with which Wu Hall demands our acknowledgment of both present and past conventions carries over into the building's interior. In the main entry hall (Figure 159), we are simultaneously confronted with the flattened ghost of Gothic stair balustrades past (Figure 160), brought forward in history, at least in profile, through the way station of Lutyens (Figure 161), to their present silhouette form at Wu Hall. The historical shadow cast by this form is made all the more poignant by its mirror image opposite—cast yet one step further forward in time, to the present. This last step in the process of historical extrusion set before us in this staircase is literally just that— a stainless-steel pipe extrusion. The ship's rail, first transformed into architecture in the 1920s through Le Corbusier's analogies to ships (Figure 162) and later rendered a conven-

155. Venturi, Rauch and Scott Brown, Gordon Wu Hall, Princeton University, Princeton, New Jersey, 1980–83. Longitudinal section. 156. Robert Smythson, Burton Agnes Hall, Yorkshire, England, 1601–10. 157. Edwin Lutyens, Little Thakeham, Sussex, England, 1902. 158. Robert Smythson, Wooton Lodge, Stratfordshire, circa 1608.

158

157

159

160

161

163

tional element in stair design by safety and handicap codes, is here exposed as a form of contemporary convention: the pipe rail—a part of life. While ascending the stair on the right we grasp cold, modern pipe. While descending, we steady ourselves with the warmth cast through the wood of English tradition. Venturi did not want the pipe rail—building codes forced it upon him. It is significant, however, that his integration of it into the design forces us to accept both. The presence of the silhouetted wood balustrade poses questions about the nature of contemporary convention even while the pipe rail draws attention to its conventional antecedents on the opposite rail. Both the past and present can be seen as rhetorical modifiers, with the content existing in the rhetorical dialogue itself.

The stainless-steel coat hooks on the oak paneled wall in the main entry hall (Figure 163) bear further witness to Wu Hall's thoroughgoing conversation between conventions past and present. The paneling, although lighter than that of Elizabethan and Gothic halls, refers to tradition. The stainless-steel hooks are off-the-rack from the local hardware store. Each is a form of convention: the paneling attains the status of custom by virtue of its pastness, while the hook rises to a comparable position through its mass-produced, object-type presence in contemporary life. The hook rhetorically gestures to and points at the paneling and vice versa. Each, by juxtaposition, elevates the other.

We at last arrive at the empty frame above the fireplace in the second-floor lounge of Wu Hall (Figure 164). The image in this frame is simply that of the wall itself . . . or is it? Can there be an image in this empty frame? Many architects would today think that question rhetorical. Thomas Cole's famous painting, *The Architect's Dream* (Figure 65), has become an af-

162

159. Venturi, Rauch and Scott Brown, Gordon Wu Hall, Princeton University, Princeton, New Jersey, 1980–83. Main stair and hall. 160. Sanderson Miller, Pomfret Castle, London, England, 1760. Staircase. 161. Edwin Lutyens, Copse Hall, Upper Slaughter, Gloucester, England, 1906. Staircase. 162. Le Corbusier, Villa Savoie, Poissy, France, 1928–30. Rail of upper ramp. 163. Venturi, Rauch and Scott Brown, Gordon Wu Hall, Princeton University, Princeton, New Jersey, 1980–83. Stainless-steel coat hooks in hall.

165

firmative vision of the past brought forward in its entirety (or near entirety) to the present, and inserted in the empty frame. Smythson's fireplace overmantle (Figure 165) with its heraldic arms in the frame lifted intact, or nearly intact, is at present an often embraced solution. On the other hand, others continue to resist even the presence of the reference to tradition posed by the frame itself. Venturi, by contrast, asks us to accept both: the rhetorical dialogue between traditional and contemporary constructive and associative conventions becomes the image—the substance—in the empty frame. Forever trapped between the demands of modern form and construction and the return to the nostalgic vocabularies of past form lifted whole, it is neither a pretty nor an easy picture. The building makes us work to understand it. Like Renaissance architecture, its meaning is enhanced by a recognition of the conventions and precedents upon which it is based. As Eliot said, tradition "cannot be inherited . . . if you want it, you must obtain it by great labour."

Having put forth the labor Eliot asks of us to decode the rhetorical dialogue between Wu Hall's multiple traditions, we are both rewarded and challenged. The reward is in the recognition of an architecture based on a relative or contingent epistemology. At Wu Hall, classical, Gothic, modern, and other forms relevant to the institution, place, and time assume a simultaneous and self-conscious currency. It is the pluralist dream: the challenge that the systematic and meaningful drawing together of diverse traditions at Wu Hall relates to the pluralist dream itself. If one measure of reality, either biological or systematic, is the ability to give rise to new forms and systems, then the pluralist dream must evolve into a specie or species in its own right, capable of generating succeeding forms through yet further recombination and development. Two as yet unanswered questions posed by pluralist form concern its epistemology and pragmatics. Can a contingent artifact that derives its meaning largely by reference to previous normative systems attain procreative status comparable to that of the

historic systems to which it alludes? While it is arguable that normative traditions, such as the classical and the Gothic, drew upon diverse, preexisting systems for the substance of their language and continually enriched that language by skillful contamination, pluralist theory is certainly different in kind—both more diverse and without any as yet apparent dominant baseline of form. Second, on a practical level, how many allusive layers can be added to a form before its meaning becomes obscure? While Wu Hall consummates many of the theoretical propositions posed fifteen years earlier in *Complexity and Contradiction,* the real measure of the building's success and its paternity lies in the difficulty of the questions it leaves us.

Notes

1. Alan Chimacoff and Alan Plattus, "Learning from Venturi," *Architectural Record* (September 1983): 86–96.

2. Reyner Banham, *Theory and Design in the First Machine Age* (New York: Praeger Publishers, 1960), pp. 241–46.

3. Robert Venturi, *Complexity and Contradiction in Architecture* (New York: Museum of Modern Art, 1966), p. 44.

4. *Ibid.,* p. 30.

5. *Ibid.,* p. 19.

6. "The Lovesong of J. Alfred Prufrock," *T. S. Eliot: Collected Poems 1909–1962* (New York: Harcourt, Brace & World, Inc., 1963), p. 6. I owe a debt here to Sanda Iliescu, who called my attention to the correlation between the specific tactics employed by Eliot in this poem and the architecture of Venturi, Rauch and Scott Brown.

164. Venturi, Rauch and Scott Brown, Gordon Wu Hall, Princeton University, Princeton, New Jersey, 1980–83. Lounge with fireplace and overmantle.   165. Robert Smythson, Bolsover Castle, Derbyshire, England, 1612–14. Chimneypiece.

Index of Proper Names and Works